CONTENTS

INTRODUCTION

This volume comprises papers given at the Baptist Historical
Society Summer School at St Edward's, Malvern, in July 1982,
on "Baptists in the Twentieth Century". As such, it consti-
tutes the most substantial publication to date on British Baptists in the modern period. This does not of course make it a
"history" of modern Baptists in Britain, for that would imply
both a greater comprehensiveness in the ground covered, and a
more unified perspective overall, whereas these papers are
written by authors working quite independently on specific
topics and questions. "Papers *Towards* Twentieth Century Baptist History" might therefore be a more accurate, as well as
more modest, title. Nevertheless, this volume is offered in
the hope of its being a significant source of information and
observation to the specialized historian and the more general
reader alike. Indeed, it may be fairly claimed that the very
diversity of these papers brings particular angles of the
modern Baptist story into much sharper focus than would be
possible for a single author at this stage.

In fact, the papers fall into two broad categories. There
are those which focus in some way or other on the life and work
of the local church, which is where a truly Baptist interest
must obviously lie. The other group deals with the wider relationships of Baptists, to their social and political environment in twentieth century Britain, to the traumas of Europe in
the first half of the century, and to the ecumenical movement.

In the first category, Dr Leonard Champion gives a charac-
teristically lucid and perceptive survey, from his personal
experience, of some of the major developments in the life of
the local church over the past fifty years or so, and carefully
weighs the gains and losses. Moving on to a more sociological
plane, David Watts provides a short but illuminating analysis
of changes in numerical strength and location of Baptist
churches in one particular urban area - Glasgow - this century.
Such surveys are highly necessary if we are to penetrate the
realities behind such slick terms as "growth" and "decline",
and it would be very useful if other cities in the United Kingdom could be surveyed in similar fashion. Then, with worship
being at the very heart of local church life, it is good to
have Michael Walker's expertly informed and trenchantly expressed insights into recent changes and developments in practice and understanding of worship, prayer and spirituality as
a whole. The subject of the final paper in the volume, Clyde
Binfield's survey of Baptist architecture around the turn of
the century, may not at first strike some readers as being of
central importance. Yet theological understanding of the
nature of worship and the divine-human encounter, of the nature
of the church and its ministry, is for good or ill conveyed by
buildings no less than by sermons and hymns, and we do well to
appreciate more deeply the non-verbal language of the architecture in which so many Baptists have been immersed this century
- even if (and perhaps *because*) the definitive forms of much
of our architecture arose during the late Victorian age.
Binfield's article incidentally emphasizes and illuminates a

2   BAPTISTS IN THE 20TH CENTURY

vital aspect of Baptist and other nonconformist life over the
past century - its social sub-culture at the level of business
and commercial interests, and above all at the level of marry-
ing and being given in marriage.

In the second category, Roger Hayden's account of J. H.
Shakespeare takes us back to the figure who decisively shaped
the structure of the Baptist Union for the twentieth century,
whose ecumenical vision failed to capture the denomination yet
still presents us with unanswered questions about the relevance
of denominationalism in a world whose spiritual anguish finds
so much intra-ecclesiastical debate less than trivial. Use-
fully, this paper points out that Shakespeare's intense concern
for re-structuring the Baptist denomination, and his later concern for church unity, were not contradictory in the light of
his one overriding concern, that of mission. Taking us still
further afield into the world of ecumenism, Dr Morris West
gives a comprehensive survey of Baptist involvement in the work
of the Faith and Order Commission since the inception of its
work at Lausanne in 1927. Here it is made clear that, on the
one hand, Baptists have been involved as leaders in some of
the most important gatherings and committees, and on the other
hand that the issue of baptism itself has become of progres-
sively more central interest and concern in this stream of the
ecumenical movement. But Baptists have of course also had to
respond to the social and political context in which they have
lived. David Bebbington, already well known for his work on
nonconformity and politics, takes us through the main changes
in Baptist political and social commitments this century, notably the breakdown of identification between the denomination
and the Liberal Party. Finally, unless something even more
hideous happens in the next seventeen years, the modern age in
European history will be stigmatized as the age of Hitler and
Nazism, and some of the most pertinent questions of the church
historian will concern the Christian response to that evil.
Keith Clements's paper on British Baptists' attitudes to the
Nazi regime, and to the dilemma of their fellow-Baptists in
Germany, attempts to add some further contours to our understanding of an episode to which we have perhaps still fully to
come to terms.

The justification for an interest in history which is other
than purely academic is that in order to know who we are, we
need to know where we have come from. These essays should
help to convince the Baptists among their readers that although
recent, their twentieth century story is as much to be considered as their "heritage" as the age of Helwys, or Carey, or
Spurgeon. It may at times appear to be less glamorous, less
successful, as a story of achievement. But the twentieth century has been an age of frightening complexity and change, and
the evaluation of Christian response to those changes will depend upon one's more basic criteria as to how the quality of
local church life is to be measured, what is involved in "witnessing" in an increasingly secularized society, and what are
the signs of the kingdom of God in the church, or world, or
both?

This is an opportune point to make an urgent plea from the
point of view of historical research. Many individuals and
churches are now familiar with the practice of depositing
their old records, minute books, letters etc., in the safe
keeping of county archivists and the like, and with the need
to be much more alert to the danger of losing valuable historical material through sheer neglect. It needs to be said
that this danger applies no less to twentieth-century material
than to the more antiquated. Indeed, several of the authors
of the papers in this volume will be able to testify to the
extraordinary difficulty to be experienced in finding primary
sources for the modern period. Much of the personal correspondence and papers of leading figures at the turn of the
century seems to have gone for ever. It is to be hoped that
the sheer volume of paper-work that we make for ourselves
today will not lead to an over-casual attitude towards what
future historians will want to read for themselves. At the
local church level, for example, it means ensuring that a
complete file of the church magazine is preserved.

In the meantime, the Baptist Historical Society is grateful
to be able to present this volume, which it is hoped will
serve the interests of all who, in whatever way or at whatever
level, have an interest in the Baptist past. For some it will
recall much within living memory. For others, some of the
scenes painted will seem like another world, such has been the
pace of change. But those who have written trust that all who
read may find the recent story as absorbing as they themselves
have felt it to be, and that where, as will sometimes be
inevitable, writers and readers differ in their conclusions,
the end result will be a still deeper and more widespread
interest in the issues which faced, and still face, this
branch of the Christian church.

K. W. C.
February 1983

BAPTIST CHURCH LIFE IN THE TWENTIETH CENTURY

SOME PERSONAL REFLECTIONS

My first purpose in this paper is to outline some changes in
Baptist church life during the past 60 years. I confine my
outline to this period because it is generally acknowledged
that the 1914-18 war marked the dividing line between one era
in western civilisation and the era in which we now live, so
a period of 60 years is an appropriate space of time. It
also happens that I was baptized just 60 years ago so that
my outline of changes is based on personal experience and
recollection.

But I have a second purpose. I want to consider the significance of the changes which I have experienced. This evaluation derives not just from personal experience but also
from two other sources. One source is found in my 21 years
of teaching in the College and the University in Bristol,
specialising in New Testament. This teaching was not based
on a denominational position but on the objectivity with
academic work. The other source is found in my association
with Christians of other countries, cultures and traditions
chiefly through my sharing in the work of the World Council
of Churches from 1954 to 1972; this gave me an appreciation
of the experiences and emphases in many other Christian communities. Thus from two points of view I have been able to
look at my experience as a committed Baptist as it were from
the outside.

Now I turn to the question: What has happened in Baptist
church life during the past 60 years?

A. THE CHANGES

First, I emphasize that amid many changes we can recognise a
spiritual continuity. Church life is still the realm in which
the presence of the living Christ is experienced, people respond to him in faith and are nurtured and supported in that
faith amid the varying experiences which the years bring to
them. So our church life is constantly marked by personal
devotion to Christ, by enriching and supportive fellowship
and by generous and useful service. This spiritual continuity
is important and must be remembered as we consider so many
changes.

1. Statistics

I begin my account of changes with some undeniable facts.
In 1921 there were 3068 churches in the Baptist Union with a
total membership of 442,000; in 1981 there were 2058 churches
with a total membership of 170,000. A 57% decline in membership. In 1921 our Sunday Schools had 518,000 scholars; in
1981, 157,000: a decline of 70%

I tested these figures against those of the Bristol Association, which for 300 years has been one of the strong centres of Baptist church life. The figures for the 50 years
from 1932 to 1981 show a decline of members from 11,000 to
5,800 i.e. 47%. And Sunday Schools from 13,000 to 3,400, a
decline of 74%.

To these sobering figures a further fact must be added.
When I entered college in 1926 my home church at Horfield,
Bristol had 821 members, and 910 Sunday School teachers and
scholars. The average morning congregation numbered 500 to
600 and the evening congregation about 1,100, i.e. there were
many regular attenders who were not members; they represented
a potential source of converts as did the Sunday School. Horfield is still one of our strongest churches with 528 members.
But the average morning congregation is some 400 and the evening some 200, with a Sunday School of 238. Our congregations
are now much more restricted to members with a small number
of people who share regularly in the fellowship without becoming members.

Early in this century when the population of our country
numbered about 40 millions the total Baptist community numbered about one million. Today the total Baptist community
numbers less than half a million in a population of over 50
millions.

2. Youth Work

Youth work has been a prominent feature of church life
throughout this century. When I went to Rugby in 1938 I found
a flourishing Sunday School of about 400 members fully graded
according to the principles developed by the Sunday School
Union. Many of the teaching staff had passed through a two
year training course in biblical knowledge, teaching method
and child psychology given by two members of the church. Most
of the teachers were members of the church and most of those
in the training course became members. All were expected to
attend the weekly preparation class. Such a Sunday School
offering to dozens of young people a lively fellowship with
many worthwhile activities could be found in many churches.

What was noticeable about this and other youth organisations
such as the Christian Endeavour societies which flourished in
numerous churches, or the Girls' Auxiliary to the B.M.S. which
was so successful for a generation, was the manner in which
young people acquired knowledge of church life and were prepared for work in it. This work in local churches was strengthened by the varied and well attended summer schools arranged
by both the B.U. and the B.M.S. It must now be admitted that
all this has greatly diminished and some of it has disappeared
altogether.

Between the wars youth clubs for young people associated
with the church were developed. Since the Second World War
many open youth clubs have appeared, squashes and other ex-
perimental youth activities have been formed. These are often
attempts to make contact with young people outside the church
and to influence them by personal association.

The many interesting activities developed in the schools
and the varied leisure pursuits now available for young people
as well as the general mental and moral climate of our society
have combined to make youth work in the churches much more
difficult and at the same time, in spite of the fine and devoted service given by many of our members, often we do not

have a sufficient number of people equipped with adequate
knowledge and experience together with the right temperament
for effective youth work.

3. Worship

The centre of all church life is worship. Amid so many
changes the times of our worship remain unaltered. Between
the wars patterns of worship began slowly to change. Ministerial behaviour and dress were still fairly formal. The
wearing of gowns became popular and some choirs were thus
arrayed. There should now be many such garments available
secondhand, for ministers appear in all kinds of dress and
choirs have almost had their day and ceased to be.

Until the 1950s morning services were attended largely by
members and offered opportunities for a teaching ministry.
Children's addresses had become customary early in the century;
there were still some morning Sunday Schools and then came the
League of Young Worshippers. Evening services had a much
stronger evangelistic emphasis and it was normal for the witness of baptism to take place in the evening.

Liturgical prayers came into gradual use and ministers'
manuals and books of prayers began to appear. M. E. Aubrey
published a Minister's Manual in 1927 and Tait Patterson's
Call to Worship, published about the same time, was quite
widely used. The culmination of such books in traditional
format and language was perhaps the manual published by E. A.
Payne and S. F. Winward in 1960.

Since the 1950s much of this has changed. Afternoon Sunday
Schools have largely disappeared. Mornings have brought family
services and evening congregations have become small. The atmosphere is usually more informal. Many translations of Scripture are used. The language and style of prayer has changed.
Members of the congregation often participate. The personal
attitude of the minister is more influential so that in enter-
ing a Baptist church other than that in which one is accustomed to worship one doesn't know what to expect.

To those who appreciate novelty all this is welcome; to
others it is disturbing. To some churches it brings freshness
and vitality; to others it means restlessness and dissension.
The regular pattern of worship which obtained in the first
half of this century afforded stability, security, peace. The
experiments and changes of recent decades have given to some
a sense of relevance and meaning, have demonstrated the adap-
tability of the faith but have weakened a feeling of coherence
in Baptist witness.

4. The Ministry

Many changes have occurred in regard to the Ministry.
During my years as a student the function of the minister
could be quite clearly defined. He was appointed to lead the
worship of the church which he did exclusively, though one or
two deacons would always lead the prayers at Communion; in
his conduct of worship he was essentially the preacher so that
visitors to a church might say that they had come to hear Mr

So-and-So. He exercised pastoral care by regular visitation of members of his congregation. He was the acknowledged leader in the life of the church. His work centred in and often was largely confined to his local church.

In recent decades these clear-cut functions have been subject to changing emphases. Ministry has been interpreted as the ministry of the whole church so that the full-time minister is seen as an "enabler"; his task is to enable the whole church to fulfil its ministry. So lay people are asked to participate in all aspects of the church's life and constantly urged to fulfil their role in the church's mission. This doesn't seem to me such a new concept when I recall the talented and stalwart lay people who exercised so much leadership in our churches in a former generation. But it has clouded our understanding of the meaning of ministry and diminished the significance of the minister's place in the life of the church.

A second emphasis has been upon areas of need in the community. Many churches now make vigorous attempts both to discern needs and then to find ways of meeting them. This has extended the function of the minister who is often the leader in such humanitarian and social work. So he becomes more of a public figure in the town in which he ministers and thereby is involved in its social concerns.

A third change is to be seen in the growth of association and denominational activities. Committees, conferences, assemblies, projects have proliferated and the conscientious minister feels that he should share in some of these activities. So the range of his functions has widened and thereby the time spent away from the concerns and needs of his local church has increased.

These changing emphases have brought a measure of uncertainty and confusion in regard to the function of the minister. At the same time there has been manifest within the ministry a changing spirit. Let me say at once that ministers at the present time seem to me as devoted and as hardworking as ministers of a previous generation, and this in spite of the more complicated and often discouraging situation in which they work. There is no lack of faith! But there has been a growth of what, with some hesitation, I call professionalism. There is a much keener awareness of the conditions of work, of hours on duty and time off, of attendance at conferences and sabbaticals, of housing and pensions. The prominence given to such matters is an indication both of the nature of the environment in which we are all living and of changing attitudes in the ministry.

5. Relationships between local churches

This brings me to the complicated theme of relationships between local churches in the life of the denomination. The traditional Baptist emphasis upon the absolute autonomy of the local church still largely obtained in the early part of the century in spite of the work and influence of leaders such as J. H. Shakespeare. Growing up in a city with many

Baptist churches I accepted that they were there. I was interested to visit some of them as opportunity offered, but
my life was in my own church. The local church was self-
sufficient and independent. This was a typical attitude at
that time, and is still not unknown. This attitude made the
movement of ministers haphazard, often dependent on personal
contacts. College principals and ministers of the larger
churches were influential persons in this process.

This century has witnessed both the growth of denominational awareness and the development of denominational organisation. Books like H. W. Robinson's *Life and Faith of the
Baptists* (1927) and W. T. Whitley's *History of British Baptists* (1923) promoted denominational awareness. During my
five years in Bristol College I cannot recall any courses on
Baptist history or beliefs. When I was interviewed for the
B. U. Scholarship in 1931, I think it was Dr Whitley who commented that my examination paper on Baptists indicated that
I knew little of European Baptists. That was true, so I replied that if granted the scholarship enabling me to spend
two years in Germany no doubt I should learn much about them.
There is, I think, now a much stronger awareness of the
Baptist position.

This finds visible expression in the growth of organisation
within the Union. The raising of large sums of money has
altered the relation of minister and churches to one another
and to the Union. The Twentieth Century Fund in 1899, the
Sustentation Fund launched in 1912, increased in 1947 by the
Victory Thanksgiving Fund and named the Home Work Fund, increased again in the 1960s by the Ter-Jubilee Fund, and now,
of course, named the Home Mission Fund has strengthened the
coherence of the denomination and deepened its sense of fellowship. The superintendency, which began in 1915 and struggled for acceptance, has furthered these processes to the
benefit of ministers and churches. The Superannuation Fund,
launched in 1927 with its capital greatly increased in the
1970s, together with the Retired Ministers' Housing Association, has given greater security to ministers. These refer-
ences indicate immense changes in the relation of churches
to one another and in the fellowship of the ministers.

This growing sense of belonging together as members of the
body of Christ has been extended by the influence of the
ecumenical movement with its changing relations between the
denominations. This has caused some to hold more firmly to a
denominational position, while for others the ties have been
loosened. And the processes of change in all these relationships seem certain to continue.

6. Local church and local community

The place of the church in the local community presents
another scene of change. I recall that half a century ago
in two successive years members of Horfield, Bristol, were
Lord Mayors of the city and civic services were thus held in
our church. This was the experience of other churches. It
was common for members of our churches to serve on town and
city councils and to hold high office. I listened, too, to

many a sermon which wrestled with Christian responses to
social changes, to intellectual challenges and to moral issues.
Many a local church and its minister held a significant place
in the life of the community and was able to influence it.

We have now to accept that our place has diminished and our
influence lessened. This was illustrated for me a few months
ago when I came across the newspaper report of my induction -
or Recognition Service as it was then known - in Minehead in
1934. The report filled over half a page, giving almost ver-
batim accounts of sermon and addresses. A similar event last
year was noted just in a modest paragraph. The national mass
media, as well as the politicians, now take little note of
what Baptists say or do. Our influence upon public affairs
has become weaker.

Of course numerous churches today promote activities to
care for the elderly, open premises for play groups, are concerned about the vast problems presented by the oppressed,
the refugees and the poor in so many parts of the world. But
other people too pursue such humanitarian work. While such
matters are referred to both in prayers and in sermons, the
range of preaching seems to me now to be more restricted. It
is sometimes a retreat into the biblical world; often it is
a somewhat pietistic dealing with issues domestic to church
life.

Have our diminished place in society and the many changes
which present radical challenges to the Christian faith turned
us inwards upon ourselves and the inner concerns of our
churches? And will this process lead to a further loss of
influence?

7. Way of life

Finally in this account of changes in our church life
during the past 60 years, I want to mention a change which is
much more difficult to describe because it concerns inner
attitudes, a feeling seldom expressed since it was unself-
conscious. Looking back I realise that being a Baptist meant
sharing in a whole way of life. This life centred in the
local church which offered a wide range of spiritual, intellectual and social activities, giving one a place in a lively
fellowship. But the church was linked with the home in many
subtle ways and both upheld certain standards which guided
both personal conduct and relationships. There was the confident feeling that this way of life was shared by many people,
that it was a worthy and satisfying way of life and that it
made a good contribution to society. One shared this way of
life with the sense of belonging to a large and vigorous
community found everywhere in our nation.

I do not think that many would now describe church life in
these terms. The interests of people are now more varied and
dispersed; they share in many more social and cultural activities outside the church. Being a Baptist now, even where
convictions are clearly held, is likely to mean being a member
of a local Baptist church and supporting Baptist organisation
and activities, both local and denominational. One pursues

BAPTISTS IN THE 20TH CENTURY

these religious activities among many other activities and though they are felt to be significant they can no longer be reckoned a way of life.

From this account of changes in Baptist church life I move on now to raise the question: What is the significance of these happenings?

B. SIGNIFICANCE OF CHANGES

1. Reflection of social changes

I suggest first that some of the changes I have spoken about are simply reflections, in the life of the church, of changes which have occurred in the environment.

In his six-volume *History of the Expansion of Christianity* Latourette ends each section by evaluating the influences of the church on its environment and the influences of the environment on the church. If we view the life of our churches during the past 60 years in that way we are bound to acknowledge that the influence of the environment on our church life has been far greater than the influence of our churches on society. This situation should make us face more realistically the blunt question: to what extent have our responses to changes in society been expressions of the gospel we profess, or have we allowed the changing fashions of the times to dictate our responses either through passive acquiescence or with the plea that we must be relevant?

Consider then three brief illustrations of the manner in which social changes have affected our church life.

(i) The changed habits of people in regard to Sunday have compelled us to abandon our Sunday afternoon schools. Looking back on the Sunday School movement which for more than a century formed such a vigorous element in the life of our churches, offering a constant opportunity for evangelism and education, one is bound to reflect that this radical change in church life has never been fully assessed. We have simply continued our traditional one hour of Sunday morning worship, linking the Sunday School with it and giving it the new name of family worship. In my judgment there is clear need for much more thought and action so that we may more adequately educate each younger generation in regard to the Christian faith and life, and bring them to an understanding and wholehearted response to Christ.

(ii) Contemporary forms of music, singing and dancing have become familiar to all of us through radio and television, discs and cassettes. The focal point of all this is in discos with their atmosphere of noise, informality and freedom. These are powerful influences upon the younger generation. To what extent has this brought changes in the methods of our children's and youth work? And a more serious question! How far are some of the changes occurring in our worship just an echo in the realm of religion of patterns of entertainment fashioned in the secular realm? And is the theological language which we attach to these experiments a means of avoiding the sharp challenge of the situation and of hiding from ourselves the real nature of what is happening?

(iii) During this century our society has been affected by the
vast increase of organisation and the growth of bureaucracy.
To organise, to plan, to appoint commissions and produce documents, to hold conferences and make speeches, to multiply officials and forms, all this has characterised 20th century
society. The emergence of departments of sociology in most
of our universities and polytechnics is a sign of the times.
And the church, including our denomination, has shown similar
characteristics. Are they marks of health or symptoms of
disease? Anyhow, does this belong to the gospel or to the
fashion of our times?

Now I am not suggesting that all this is wrong. The church
must live in its immediate environment and be responsive to
its changes, though as Baptists we are bound to qualify such
a statement when we recall the emphasis which our spiritual
forefathers placed upon the separation of the church from the
world, with the people of God as a community gathered out of
the world and, like Abraham, seeking a city which has founda-
tions whose builder and maker is God.

An issue of the *Times Literary Supplement* last February
carried a review of D. W. Bebbington's book *The Nonconformist
Conscience*. The review ended with these words "... the nonconformist Conscience belonged to an age which was distinguished for its faith, its lively provincialism and its optim-
istic individualism. It perished at the hands of those three
all consuming ogres of 20th century Britain, secularism, sub-
urbanism and socialism". That expresses sharply my argument
in offering my three illustrations. Some important changes
in our church life have been allowed to occur through the
pressures of a secular environment and without sufficient reflection as to whether they are in conformity with the nature
of the gospel. But this raises another important issue.

2. Need for clearer theological direction

What I wish to stress now is that the changes we have experienced have brought about an urgent need for clearer theological direction.

The structures of Baptist church life built up during the
17th century were based on a firm and definite theological
foundation. The inner Lordship of Christ and the external
authority of Scripture constituted the basis on which were
formulated patterns of worship in which the ministry of the
Word was pre-eminent, an understanding of baptism was developed as the personal commitment of faith involving specific
forms of personal behaviour, and an emphasis was made upon
the obligation of membership in a gathered community of believers. Here was a coherence of belief and practice. This
unity of doctrine and life was maintained during the process
of renewing and enlarging of church life which occurred at
the end of the 18th and the early part of the 19th centuries
under the influence of Fuller, Ryland and other leaders. They
perceived fresh implications of the basic position and this

led to the new efforts in evangelism at home and abroad, to
the formation of the BMS and the BU, and to increasing involvement in social and national affairs.   In all these
changes the coherence of doctrine and practice remained
largely intact.

This is no longer the position.   Just as social changes
have affected the life of our churches, so the theological
changes of this century have exercised diverse and divergent
influences.   In an era in which we have needed a strong
foundation of clear and relevant beliefs, we have been caught
up in a bewildering variety of movements, shifts and at times
temporary fashions in theological thinking.

Critical work on the nature and documents of the Bible
during the past 100 years, the social and humanitarian emphasis of liberal theology, the absolutes and paradoxes of
Barthianism, the grappling with the ethical dilemmas inherent
in a technological society with Tillich, Niebuhr and Bonhoeffer, the charismatic movement with its emphasis on the Spirit
and spiritual gifts, liberation theology - listening to questions raised by new orders of society - these constantly
changing influences have caused considerable theological uncertainty and confusion.

All these emphases have been represented among us, some
settling for one position, others for other positions.   Some
have reacted to all this with a mild interest sufficient to
make debating points in ministers' fraternals, but in fact
continuing to speak and act in the life of the church as if
these theological changes had not really happened, so adopting a kind of implicit fundamentalism.   Others reject these
changes because they hold a genuine fundamentalist position.

Even where some attempts have been made both to clarify
a theological position and to perceive its implications, the
issues have been largely confined to the inner affairs of the
church.   So we have had reports on ordination, on ministry,
on baptism and the Lord's Supper, on the Associations.   It
was right to think about these issues both for the sake of
our churches and for our ecumenical relationships, but these
are not the radical issues which face the Christian faith
today. These do little to help us weather the intellectual
and social storms which are falling upon both our society and
our churches.

So the coherence of belief and structure, the unity of
doctrine and practice, which was evident in the origin of
Baptist churches and in which churches lived for some 300
years until the early part of this century, has now been
broken.   Yet this coherence is essential for vital fellowship
and effective witness.

So I stress our need for clearer theological direction.
This is not a plea for more academic theology.   In my judgment much academic theology of the 20th century has been the
esoteric pursuit of professionals, unrelated to the needs of
a witnessing church or to the human situation with which believers are striving to cope.   In Ernest Payne's translation

of an Anabaptist hymn is the prayer "We seek fresh guidance from Thy Word, now grant anew Thy blessing". Placing a wider interpretation upon those words we can suggest that what we need and should be seeking is fresh guidance from God's Word which is Jesus Christ for a powerful, contemporary formulation of the gospel, which would provide the content for our communication of the faith, create the impetus for our mission, sustain us amid the radical challenges we all face and offer guidance for fresh patterns and activities in our churches. So we should be led into a new coherence of doctrine and practice. That would indeed be a rich blessing.

3. Response to radical questions

This brings me to my final point. Here I make the judgment that the changes in our church life this century have not been a wholly adequate response to the radical questions with which our total situation has been facing us. Let me offer some evidence for the judgment.

The Baptist position was founded and has been largely maintained upon a view of the nature and authority of Scripture which the results of biblical scholarship and of a more sensitive appreciation of the work of the Holy Spirit in the traditions of all the churches make it difficult to hold. We have not really come to terms with this position. If we are to maintain the Baptist distinctives, we need to establish them in a more comprehensive biblical and theological foundation which will justify our position, and at the same time make clear what is valid in traditions other than ours, so offering guidance for our relationships with them. Here are radical questions about the authority for the Baptist position which have not been fully met.

Again, the Baptist position was founded and has been largely maintained in opposition to other ecclesiastical beliefs and practices. The account of the origins of Dissent in the Broadmead Records portrays a progressive rejection of aspects of the established church and a developing withdrawal into a dissenting position. This attitude persisted and was prevalent still in the early part of this century. Baptists looked at other denominations from a Baptist point of view which was accepted as the biblical position and therefore as the most valid position. So the degrees of rejection ranged from mild interest in the other Free Churches, though union with them which was one of the aims of the Free Church Council was not thought possible, to opposition to episcopacy, struggle against the privilege of establishment and hatred of the papacy. This is no longer the situation. We can no longer validate our position over against the position of others or by rejection of them. A leading article in *The Times* recently commented upon the changed relationships between the denominations in general and upon the work of the theological commission of the Church of England and the Roman Catholic church in particular, and ended with the statement that the work of the commission "beautifully exemplifies and advances that courtesy, charity and respect between Christians of different denominations which to many minds is the sweetest fruit of the ecumenical movement". This situation is addressing radical questions to us about the spirit and manner in which we are to maintain a Baptist position, about the relationships with other Christian communities which we should cultivate, and about the judgment which the gospel exercises both upon all denominational positions and upon the manner in which they are maintained.

Again, the Baptist position was founded and has been maintained in an environment in which the Christian understanding of the nature of the universe and of life was widely accepted, so that denominational positions could be upheld without affecting the general position of the Christian faith in society. This is no longer the situation. Contemporary views about the origin and nature of the universe, about the constitution and destiny of man, about human society and its purpose, do not question a denominational position; they are powerful elements in an environment which questions the fundamental beliefs held by all Christians. We are moving into an era in which denominational differences will appear increasingly irrelevant. Already numbers of church members move easily from one denomination to another when they change their place of living, for they feel that their allegiance is to the basic Christian belief and practice which all churches advocate and not to a denominational position. I do not discern in our denomination a clear awareness of this radical situation in which we are all placed or of its implications for us.

I have mentioned three realms in which radically new questions are being addressed to us. What is significant is that all this is occurring at one and the same time. We are being beset on every side.

When I was a student in the 1920s we often quoted in our sermons the words of Rupert Brooke written during the 1914-18 war. "Now God be thanked who has matched us with His hour". We can perhaps excuse exuberant and confident youth making that somewhat arrogant assertion. It would have been better had we prayed for wisdom to understand the changing times in which we were living and grace to bring to those changes the light and power of the gospel. I think that we served our churches and our times faithfully but not as wisely and as courageously as we should. So I pray that the God who makes all things new will find a more adequate response in the generation which is now shaping our church life.

L. G. CHAMPION

BAPTISTS IN GLASGOW

THE TWENTIETH CENTURY CHALLENGE

OF URBAN GROWTH AND DECLINE

INTRODUCTION

It cannot be said that the West of Scotland, or Scotland in general, forms a historic Baptist heartland. The first churches had their origins only in the mid 18th century, firstly in Keiss, Caithness (1750), and then Glasgow and Edinburgh (in the 1760s). From these late beginnings, however, a widespread movement in the early 19th century compensated to a degree for early absence. Scottish Baptists can now be found from Shetland to Stranraer, Islay to Hawick.

During the early 19th century, the one 18th century foundation in Glasgow (George Street) became seven by evangelism and division. By 1862 there were:-

  2 "Scotch" Baptist churches* (John Street and Brown Street).
  1 "English" Baptist church (Hope Street, later Adelaide Place).
  4 Undefined (S. Portland Street, Blackfriars Street – later John Knox Street, Frederick Street – later Dennistoun, and Cambridge Street).

These were all located in the core of the City (what is now the "Central Area"). Membership totalled about 1000 in a City of 395,500 at the 1861 census.

THE VICTORIAN CITY (1860 - World War I)

Urban Growth **

Glasgow in 1861 was a city of squares and tenements developed in Georgian/Regency style, mostly to the north of the River Clyde in an elegant and pleasant fashion, apart from the warrens of the medieval High Street area. Between 1861 and World War I it exploded in size, extending tentacles into the surrounding countryside north and south, developing first satellites, then swallowing up small towns such as Scotstoun, Partick, Maryhill, Springburn, Shettleston, Calton, Rutherglen, Shawlands, Pollokshields and Govan. This building boom was based on a tremendous growth in industry - shipbuilding, heavy engineering, textiles, clothing, railway engines, food and

---

* These were organised differently from a usual Baptist church of the time, with a plurality of pastors, a body of deacons, breaking of bread each Lord's Day, the Love Feast, congregational prayers and exhortations, unanimity of decisions in the church meeting, washing of feet etc. These characteristics arose from Glasite or Sandemanian origins.

** See map, page 20

drink, chemicals. The city grew to a size of 1,034,000 by
1921, 2½ times the size of its population of 1861.

What of the Baptists?

Growth of the fellowship of believers in the City grew five-
fold. The 7 churches of 1861 became 17 in 1914 (plus six
mission halls). Growth patterns are of considerable interest,
they were as follows:-

    i) Four of the "old" central churches remained broadly
       static in size and rebuilt their churches (John Knox
       Street, Adelaide Place, Cambridge Street, John Street).

   ii) Three churches moved from the central core and grew
       rapidly in adjacent suburbs (Brown Street to Bridgeton,
       Frederick Street to Dennistoun, South Portland Street
       to Victoria Place, Gorbals).

  iii) The "old" churches developed branch missions which
       mostly then became fully constituted independent chur-
       ches (Govan, Kelvinside and Hillhead). One - Hillhead -
       developed a "daughter" church quite quickly at Partick
       and two missions in another part of Partick and at Port
       Dundas. These all experienced rapid growth in member-
       ship.

   iv) Spontaneous groupings of Baptists resident in the "new"
       more affluent suburbs formed independent fellowships
       which proceeded to grow quickly   (Queen's Park,
       Shettleston, Rutherglen, Cambuslang).

    v) In the poorer districts of the growing City, missions
       led by charismatic ministers or church planters
       developed into constituted churches and then lost
       impetus (Harper Memorial church in Tradeston - John Harper,
       Springburn - J. Horne, Hutchesontown - C. S. Donald,
       Whiteinch - the Pioneer Mission).

All these changes arose from a massive co-operative effort of
visitation, open air meetings, Sunday School work, tract distribution, and fund raising. It resulted in a membership of
5518 in 1921 and a network of churches across the city, but it
must be said that Baptists were far stronger in the areas of
middle class Glasgow - the West End and South Side.

INTER-WAR   GLASGOW

Urban Trends

Glasgow experienced a boom in employment during the first
World War and through the reconstruction phase, as its indus-
tries provided for defence needs. 1921, however, brought an
era of permanent depression and high unemployment. Population
growth halted.

    Urban growth, however, continued through a spreading of
population from inner Glasgow to new overspill suburbs. These
were developed by the Corporation to relieve the inner slums
(notably Knightswood on the west, Possil Park on the north,

various schemes on the east side, Mosspark on the southwest)
and by private builders in the 1930s to meet new demands for
owner occupation (Cathcart, Newlands, Giffnock on the south,
Kelvinside on the west, Mount Vernon on the east).

What of the Baptists?

The new era brought new trends in lifestyle, philosophy and
spiritual interest, but also economic depression brought spiritual aridity and a lack of growth. This was reflected in
the churches as follows:-

  i) The "central" churches declined, reflecting population
     dispersal.

 ii) The inner city churches in "slum areas" (Govan, Kelvin-
     side/Maryhill, Gorbals, Springburn, Shettleston, Partick)
     experienced static or declining memberships. One, the
     mission at Hutchesontown, closed.

iii) Those in more affluent areas (Hillhead, Queens Park,
     Cambuslang, Rutherglen) did better, but even so experi-
     enced little growth.

 iv) Five new churches were established, growing to a limited
     size: "Hermon" in Cathcart Road, Govanhill (a reconsti-
     tution of a mission established in the 1890s), Cathcart
     and Kings Park in the growing southern private housing
     suburbs, Mosspark and Knightswood in new better class
     Council estates on the west of the city. The latter
     emerged through co-operative efforts, with the Baptist
     Union and Glasgow Association closely involved. (No
     churches were planted on the poorer schemes in Possil
     Park or around Springburn).

In general, the churches were engaged in a holding operation
and concerned with keeping their existing fellowships together.
There was less need to build new churches since urban growth
had slackened and population growth halted. There was also
some resistance since ministers knew that new peripheral churches would sap their inner congregations of numbers since by
now they drew many members from the suburbs. Even so, in
overall terms, Baptists remained at about the same numbers by
the outbreak of the Second World War as they had at the end
of the first.

POST WAR PERIOD

Urban Trends

Another economic boom during the re-armament period and the
Second World War brought back full employment to the city.
1946 brought the return of unemployment and a slowly gathering
decline of the city's economy through the 1960s and 1970s.

     Urban change became dramatic as the Corporation supported
by heavy government subsidies pursued large re-development
programmes of the city's worst slums and huge construction
programmes of the peripheral housing estates (Drumchapel,

Castlemilk, Pollok and Easterhouse) during the 1950s and 1960s. In the 1970s policies changed to favour rehabilitation of the inner city tenement areas and improvement of the already deteriorating housing estates.   Population during the period 1946 to 1981 dropped from around one million to 740,000.

Population was also transferred out of the city to New Towns at Erskine, Cumbernauld and East Kilbride, and as private builders continued to build private estates in the suburbs surrounding the city (e.g. at Bearsden, Bishopbriggs, Kirkintilloch, Newton Mearns).

Baptist Church Responses

Decline in membership set in dramatically over the period in an atmosphere of migration, upheaval and spiritual apathy. From 5700 members in 1941, numbers in 1981 were half that: around 2800.   Decline has slowed considerably, if not slightly reversed, in recent years.

These trends have been expressed in an upheaval of the distribution of congregations as follows:-

i)   In the central area and inner slums - 7 churches closed (John Street, John Knox Street, Cambridge Street, Kelvinside, Victoria Place, Bridgeton, Whiteinch).   These were in areas most affected by population losses through redevelopment and commercial development.   Only one central church - Adelaide Place - remains (adapting its role to new approaches of ministry to students and the needy, and beginning to grow).   All inner city missions closed.

ii)   Other inner churches have continued to decline, particularly in areas affected by re-development.   Some have had closure threats but remained through a determination to survive to minister to the new re-constructed areas emerging after wholesale demolitions.

iii)   Outer suburban churches remained broadly static, their areas unaffected by change.

iv)   Eight new churches have been established.   Each of the large peripheral schemes have had churches planted through deliberate efforts co-ordinated by the Scottish Baptist Union with parent fellowships and in the burgeoning private suburbs four further fellowships have or are being built up (Bearsden, Bishopbriggs, Clarkston, and Newton Mearns) on a more independent basis.

In all cases, new churches have meant an initial rapid growth of membership, with later steadying or even decline.   The council estate churches, in particular, have found that keeping their initial momentum going has been difficult.

CONCLUSIONS

In this assessment of Baptist Church life in Glasgow as seen against the background of traumatic urban growth and change, several trends can be seen. Church planting is essential for continued growth of membership and witness. Fellowships reaching a certain size tend to stop growing. Baptist churches have tended to flourish more in the wealthier areas than in poorer areas. Higher status suburbs have tended to occasion spontaneous formation of congregations whilst deliberate efforts of planning and mission have been necessary in poorer areas. These common characteristics have lessons for the ongoing witness of the Baptists in complex urban areas in the 1980s.

DAVID WATTS

CHURCH GROWTH IN GLASGOW

BAPTIST CHURCHES FOUNDED PRE 1870 -

FOUNDATION 1870-1910 -

FOUNDED BETWEEN THE WARS -

POST WAR FOUNDATION -

DIRECT LINK IN FOUNDATION -

CLOSED - C

BAPTIST WORSHIP IN THE TWENTIETH CENTURY

At the turn of this century the Baptist denomination stood at
the peak of its strength, both numerically and in terms of its
wider influence. The pattern of its worship had been shaped
by the developments and conflicts of the nineteenth century,
a knowledge of which is essential to our understanding of the
legacy with which the present century began.

In common with other Reformation churches the Baptists of
the late eighteenth and early nineteenth centuries shaped their
worship around the twin foci of word and sacrament. The theology that most influenced them at this point was that of the
radical reformation rather than of Luther and Calvin. In so
far as they discussed the theology of worship their attention
was given to the question of who should or should not adminis-
ter word and sacrament and, a matter that occupied their ener-
gies far more, the rôle of the Lord's Supper in the discipline
of the church. On the question of ministry there was, at the
outset, general agreement that word and sacrament were a dele-
gated responsibility to be administered only by those the
church authorized. That this should be limited to the ordained
ministry was being questioned at least by 1838, when Joseph
Angus took issue with a contributor to the *Baptist Magazine*
who had averred, "Ordination does not *limit* the right to ad-
minister word and ordinances to those who receive it".[1] The
question of communion and its relationship to open and closed
membership rumbled on through the century, carried in at least
two cases beyond the province of theology to the law courts.
The *meaning* of the Lord's Supper seems to have been of little
concern. Baptists seem to have been untouched by Lutheran or
Calvinist eucharistic theologies, broadly following the memori-
alist emphasis of Zwingli.

This lack of a eucharistic theology was to be a major factor
in the direction taken by Baptists in the nineteenth century.
On the one hand, preaching became the dominant hall-mark of
their worship, on the other, the Lord's Supper, though still
faithfully observed, was over-shadowed by the pulpit.

This process was accelerated by the growing catholicity of
the Anglican church, initiated by the Tractarians, and the resurgence of Roman Catholic life in these islands. Baptist
response to these developments followed the same pattern as
that of other evangelical Christian groups and is a story in
itself. By and large, they were heartily contemptuous of
catholic Christianity and especially of the more ebullient
liturgical experiments of the Ritualist party in the Church of
England. J. H. Hinton, secretary of the Baptist Union, writing
in the *Baptist Magazine* in 1868, contrasted the moral and
spiritual motivation of the individual who had responded to
Christ with the impersonal and ceremonial character of *religion*.
This led him to the further unhappy contrast between the subjective and the sacramental. He was typical of his fellow
Baptists when he emphasized the superiority of the personal and

the subjective over against the religious and the sacramental.
Clearly, there could be no dissembling between catholics and
nonconformists. The first gloried in their objective sacramen-
talism and the second in individualist subjectivism; each considered the other's virtue as nothing less than theological vice.
The Baptist response to the theological challenge of catholicity
was defensive. They still honoured and observed the ordinance
(for some even the word "sacrament" was too much to swallow),
Spurgeon himself observing it every Lord's day.[2] It became more
and more important, however, to distance themselves from the
catholics. The Lord's Supper had to be seen to be free from all
sacramental and sacerdotal associations. It is no exaggeration
to say that some Baptists would have summed up their theology
of the sacrament by saying that it was *not* catholic. What it
was presented far more difficulties and the question went largely
unanswered apart from a few brave attempts, notably by John
Clifford.[3] Perhaps to have wrestled with its meaning would have
involved straying into alien territory. Even the Calvinist Baptists ignored Calvin when it came to eucharistic theology. So
the nineteenth century left communion honoured and observed, but
isolated from any genuinely central role in the worship of the
church.

Preaching was a different matter altogether. The nineteenth
century witnessed a golden age of Free Church preaching, in
which Baptists shared to the full. The pulpit was a powerful
medium of communication attracting to it men of immense talent.
Spurgeon was the chief luminary amongst many pulpit stars. In
1877 the *Baptist Magazine* was able to survey the galaxy, featur-
ing an appreciation of a particular preacher each month -
Alexander Maclaren, Hugh Stowell Brown, C. J. Vaughan, William
Landels, R. W. Dale, F. W. Farrar, W. M. Punshon, H. Allen,
H. P. Liddon and C. Stanford. Preaching, and the buildings
which had grown around it, formed the chief liturgical legacy
that the nineteenth century nonconformists bequeathed to the
twentieth. Long into the years of this century there continued
to be Baptist churches in which preaching was central to the
life and strength of the congregation. They attracted men who
were scholar pastors, evangelical to their core, widely read,
liberal in their politics,and radical in their sympathies. They,
and the congregations that gathered around them, are still alive
in memory - J. B. Middlebrook at New North Road, Huddersfield,
B. Grey Griffith at Tredegarville, Cardiff, H. Ingli James at
Queens Road, Coventry, and Henry Cook, minister of Ferme Park in
London to name but a few. They were men clear about their task,
their preaching borne along by the expectations of those who
came to "sit at their feet".

It was indeed a golden age of preaching, yet one doomed to
decline. Not because the men necessary for it were no longer
to be found. It was the congregations that died, not the preachers. A sermon is not something a man spins like a web out of
his own emotional and spiritual resources, it is the creation
of a congregation that by the promise of its presence calls
forth the word and waits for it to be uttered. Preaching is
dependent upon congregations that find words a natural means of
communication. Consequently, it has probably been the chief
casualty of the numerical decline of this century. In more

recent times that same decline has been responsible for siring
new forms of worship and, in some cases, desperate measures to
remedy desperate situations. Decline has been the joker in
the pack, it has both prompted brave and dangerous gambles and,
at the same time, bedevilled rational theological thought.

It was in this setting of a weakened concept of the Lord's
Supper and preaching grown powerless to stem the ebbing tide
that there emerged the movements that have most influenced our
worship in recent decades, liturgical renewal, the radicalism
of the sixties, and, most recently, the Church Growth movement.

The Liturgical Renewal

The twentieth century did not open wholly bereft of some
sense of liturgical experiment. The very architecture of some
of our chapels, built in the closing years of the nineteenth
century, betray a fascination for tractarian styles alongside
the vehement rejection of ritualist theology and practice. In
the splendid building at Christchurch, near Waterloo in South
London, F. B. Meyer encouraged a limited measure of spoken congregational response in his thoughtfully structured services.
Alas, it seems to be nowhere recorded in any detail and its
content was lost in the fires that destroyed the chapel in the
Second World War. That there was a more general move to order
and dignity in worship is evidenced by the appearance of ministers' "manuals" that gave form to the celebration of sacraments
and introduced their users to the catholic treasury of prayer.
In 1927, M. E. Aubrey published his *Minister's Manual*, a book
that was to remain in circulation for the next twenty-five
years. It provided a simple ground-plan for the observance of
the basic rites of the church. Its repertoire of prayer was
limited and such as could probably have been introduced into
churches accustomed only to extemporaneous prayer without giving
offence or evoking comment. More adventurous souls could turn
to Tait Patterson's *Call to Worship* where there was a much
fuller selection of prayers, most of them drawn from the catholic treasury of prayer.

The movement for liturgical renewal was given its chief impetus by the emergence of the ecumenical movement in the post-
war years. This coincided with the appearance of a pioneer in
our denomination who was to set the pattern and provide an example for many younger ministers during the forties and fifties.
In the unlikely setting of Highams Park, in East London, Stephen
Winward, over a period of twenty-eight years (1935-63), created
a whole new ethos of worship that was to affect congregations
far beyond his own. He re-emphasized what was, by then, the by
no means generally recognized Reformation pattern of worship as
an offering of word and sacrament. Weekly communion became the
established pattern at Highams Park, the communion being an integral part of the service and not the embarrassing addendum
that it had become in many if not most Baptist churches. In
addition, members of the congregation were involved in reading
the scriptures and offering prayer, whilst the corporate participation of the whole congregation was made possible by learned

responses following scripture readings and prayers, and the use of the Sursum Corda in communion. This patiently pursued experiment provided the background to books such as *The Reformation of Our Worship* (1964) and a prayer book for use by minister and congregation. Winward's work probably reached its widest audience when he co-operated with Ernest Payne in the compiling of *Orders and Prayers for Christian Worship* (1960). The introduction to the book was itself an education in liturgical theology, whilst the range of prayers and the order of sacramental worship drew on the wealth both of the catholic and the reformed tradition. The great eucharistic prayer included both the *anaphora*, the thanksgiving, and the *epiclesis*, the invocation of the Holy Spirit. United with the word, the sacrament had been brought back to the centre of the liturgical stage.

Winward's work was undoubtedly made more effective by the ecumenical movement. The introduction of Christians to one another and the initially novel experience of sharing in one another's worship, made people far more flexible in their approach to their own tradition. They were unable to sustain the unquestioned prejudices that had surrounded their often false conceptions of what other people's worship was about. Hostility often turned to envy. Nonconformists found the catholic that lurked in their souls and catholics explored the freedom of extemporaneous prayer. Transcendence and immediacy were introduced to each other after a long period of illegal separation.

At the local level, these developments were not, however, accompanied by any radical theological thinking. Changes in the structure of worship and the bringing of the eucharist into the heart of worship renewed people's understanding of the church and the nature of its fellowship with Christ, they did not lead to a re-appraisal of eucharistic theology. Interest centred on *lex orandi* rather than *lex credendi*. Baptists who would gladly discuss the way in which communion should be conducted remained curiously indifferent to the deeper question of what the eucharist means.

Two events, coming from oblique directions, pressed the theological question with greater urgency. First, Neville Clark published *An Approach to the Theology of the Sacraments* (1955), a work that dramatically up-graded the discussion of liturgical theology. Secondly, in the early sixties, two works on baptism, *The Biblical Doctrine of Initiation* by R. E. O. White and *Baptism in the New Testament* by G. R. Beasley-Murray, revolutionized the Baptist understanding of the initiating sacrament. The bulk of Baptist thinking on the sacraments had traditionally centred on baptism. One searches in vain for significant works on the Lord's Supper before Winward and Clark wrote their books. Yet the Baptist approach to baptism was marked by the same anti-sacramentalism that had characterized their understanding of the Lord's Supper. Some churches were not at all sure that baptism was anything more than a cosmetic addition to conversion, others held that it was necessary as an act of obedience rather than a means of grace, an ordinance rather than a sacrament, whilst it was almost

universally held to be a personal confession of faith rather
than a proclamation of the salvific acts of God in Christ, a
perfect embodiment of our extra-scriptural definition of salvation as "receiving the Lord Jesus Christ as my own, personal
saviour". Both White and Beasley-Murray took us back to the
biblical world in which no symbol is without substance and no
sign separate from that which it signifies. Of course, the
concern of neither of them was primarily liturgical. They
were dealing with theologies of the church and salvation.
Yet both brought the sacrament of baptism out of the Zwinglian
shadows and made us see that here was indeed a place of ren-
dezvous between God and man, an integral part of that process
of conversion by which a man or woman is raised from death to
life in Christ, is cleansed of sin, made a member of the body
of Christ and endowed with the gift of the Spirit.

Whether this theology has yet found adequate liturgical
expression is to be doubted. Certainly the uniting of baptism, communion and reception into membership into one liturgical act is practised in a number of our churches. But there
would still be many who see it as nothing more than an example
of liturgical exotica and happily continue to sunder conversion, baptism, communion, church membership and, more recently, the gift of the Spirit one from the other. The refusal
to see liturgy as the expression of theology, *lex orandi lex
credendi*, has meant that our best baptismal theologies have
still found no firm place in church life, with the consequence
that the Lord's Supper remains unaffected by the biblical concept of sacrament unearthed by our baptismal theologians. It
remains to be seen whether the theological impact of the
liturgical renewal passed us by, leaving us with some fragile
changes in our worship which could so easily be swept away in
some of the floods that now threaten to engulf us.

The Radical Sixties

The ecumenical movement had another spin-off in the radicalism of the sixties. Christians trying to piece together
the complicated jig-saw puzzle of faith and order began to
find more amenable points of contact in life and work. In a
world faced with desperate problems many Christians found
themselves increasingly impatient with the finer points of
liturgical theology. Other, far more pressing, matters were
to hand. Worship and theology seemed to drive Christians
apart, whereas practical involvement brought them together.
Out of common action was born common prayer.

This radicalism called into question much that had traditionally lain at the heart of the church. In his book *The
New Reformation* Bishop John Robinson extended to corporate
worship some of the notions he had first explored with reference to private prayer in his earlier book *Honest to God*
(1963). There Robinson had remarked on the growing difficulties encountered by Christians as they tried to sustain
a regular and disciplined life of prayer. Prayer, people
were saying, was a withdrawal from the world and, as such,
a withdrawal from that very sphere in which most of them

found God most real. Prayer simply created an empty and un-
inhabited space. Better far to seek God in one's neighbour,
encountering him in love, the one unconditional factor in the
Christian life. Robinson's later book applied this pattern
of occasional prayer to public worship. The weekly round of
Sunday and six working days ill-accorded with the rhythm of
modern life. Worship, he said, should be held in larger set-
tings, on special festive occasions and at more widely spaced
intervals. In reply to the question, "Why go to church?"
the radical answer was, "Yes indeed, why?".

Preaching, already affected by the numerical decline of
congregations, suffered further as a result of a loss of confidence in the ministry. Social work was taking on an unpre-
cedented importance in the life of the community, supplanting
the church from its traditional pastoral concerns. Schools
were desperately in need of teachers of religious education
and the colleges of education were expanding in what, from
the vantage point of the eighties, seems an almost unbelievable
burst of growth and vitality. For those who felt increasingly
uneasy about their ministerial vocation alternatives were
plentiful and were seen by many not so much as a defection
from the Christian ministry as an extension of it or even its
true fulfilment. The ministry of word and sacrament had constantly to defend itself against the charge of irrelevance,
in those heady days a sin worse than adultery. Preaching was
ridiculed as ineffective as a means of communication, what is
done and what is seen being far more easily understood and
retained than what is heard. Robinson dismissed the pulpit
as being "six feet above contradiction". Even the evangelicals chortled with the radicals as the evangelical poet Gordon
Bailey dismissed the pulpit as "coward's castle". Some
churches responded with experiment. People did not want to
be subject to the tyranny of the monologue, it was claimed,
so in place of the sermon were substituted group discussion,
dialogue, choral speaking and acted parables. Baptist churches probably indulged less than others in such experiments,
saved by their innate conservatism rather than any firm convictions about the value of the sermon.

Another movement of the sixties that had liturgical implications was Family Church. Aimed at introducing children to
the worshipping community of the church it came to influence
the content and style of worship. The frame-work of the
Christian Year began to figure prominently in worship, providing as it did an ideal syllabus for teaching. The great
festivals and the seasons that preceded them, such as Advent
and Lent, were marked by celebration in a way that they had
not been before. Whereas the chief motive was to make them
more meaningful to children, it also served to introduce them
to church members who had not always grasped their full significance. The presence of children also made congregational
participation easier, an activity further stimulated by the
publication of the new *Baptist Hymn Book* (1962) with its
provision for responsive readings and a small selection of
public prayers for congregational use. The lay-out of the
hymn-book itself emphasized the patterns provided by the

liturgical renewal. The Lord's Supper was given greater emphasis, its value as a visual teaching medium being grasped
by a generation newly susceptible to informed educational
opinion. Family Church, however, had its adverse effect and,
with the passing of the years, it begins to pose a threat to
the offering of word and sacrament as the central activity of
the whole congregation. The presence of children has had an
inhibiting effect on preaching. The style, admittedly influenced also by the way people communicate on television, has
changed. Instead of exploring language preachers have sought
for the lowest common denominator in the attempt to be understood. The exigencies of the Sunday morning time-table have
placed their own restrictions upon the sermon. The worst effect of Family Church is only now being seen, however. As
church attendances have dropped and evening service in many
places has dwindled to a handful of people, the dominance of
the young in the morning has become an embarrassment. The
demands made by them upon the attention and the manpower of
the church become increasingly difficult to deal with. This
is evidenced in the Sunday morning "haemorrhage" when the
bulk of those under thirty years of age leave before either
word or sacrament, depleting and weakening the church at the
point of its central act. A way has to be found of enabling
children to grow within the rich liturgical tradition of the
church without at the same time impoverishing that very tradition. In some churches the situation is desperate and beginning to verge on the ridiculous.

The last factor we must take into account when recalling
the sixties was the holding of the Second Vatican Council and
the total shift in relationships between Roman Catholics and
Christians of other persuasions. Doors were opened in a way
that would have been unimaginable to former generations and,
as a consequence, there came a new understanding of the catholic dimension in life and worship. There was at last the
possibility of a genuine rapport between protestantism and
catholicity. That rapport has not been without its critics
on both sides. Given the openness of the times it seemed
possible that Baptists might overcome their aversion to catholicity and be enriched by a tradition they had hitherto viewed
with deep suspicion. A minority were. The mood of the seventies witnessed a change, however. The heady freedom of the
sixties, refreshing as it was for many Christians, did nothing
to halt decline. Astonishingly, the pendulum swung in a conservative and more authoritarian direction. Many Baptists
turned their backs on any pilgrimage towards greater catholicity, choosing instead sectarianism.

The Charismatic Movement

It may seem strange to refer to the charismatic movement in
the context of growing conservatism. But contained in that
ebullient flood-tide or, to change the imagery, housed in that
Trojan horse, were a new breed of authoritarians come to lead
us to a style of fideism long unfamiliar to Baptists and a far
remove from the Free Church tradition in these islands. It

has itself been a sign of the times which are marked by a new
fundamentalism in many areas. It is seen in those Roman Catholics who have grown fearful of the changes initiated by Vatican Two. It is evident in a resurgent Islam that endeavours
to lead whole nations back to the purity of the Prophet's
teaching. Politics of both the right and left are more pola-
rised than at any time, rigorous in their ideologies and ob-
sessed with the minutiae of party doctrine. The eighties find
people in deep need of re-assurance and success comes to those
who can offer it, whatever the price paid in reason and mode-
ration.

The charismatic movement, strangely, received great impetus
by its appearance in the Roman Catholic church in the United
States. Its effect in that extraordinary institution was almost wholly benign, experiment being contained by structure,
individual eccentricities held by discipline and loyalty to
the whole body over-riding the spiritual insights of the few.
In Baptist churches, too, there has been enrichment as the
charismatic movement has gained ground and influenced many of
our churches in different ways. There has been a strengthening of the ecumenical dimension. Baptists encountering catholics stamped with the unmistakeable *imprimatur* of the
"second blessing" have had to consider the significance of
the eucharist for those for whom it is a focal point of their
newly discovered love for God. The charismatic movement has
also emphasised the role of the congregation in worship. This
has happened in ways more dramatic than the ordered responses
of the earlier liturgical movement. Spontaneity has given
congregations access to roles within worship that a more
tightly ordered structure seemed to deny them. There has also
been the production of new songs and hymns. Some have been
abysmal rubbish, but many haunting and beautiful. The lovely,
scriptural refrains that have risen out of charismatic worship
have brought a new dimension of freedom, have set us free from
hymn-books and delivered us from an exclusive dependence upon
church organs. They have been universal. Alleluias heard
regularly in many of our Baptist churches could be heard
rising from the vast crowds of young people that waited for
the Pope on his visit to Murrayfield Stadium during the summer
of 1982.

There has been another, less happy, side to the picture.
Our loosely knit congregations have suffered pitifully from
secessions and divisions. Of more immediate concern to our
present study has been the renunciation of biblical scholarship in favour of old-style fundamentalism. Something very
different from the conservative evangelicalism of an earlier
generation is now emerging in our midst. Even Biblical
scholars whose evangelical credentials are impeccable and
scholarship above reproach are viewed with suspicion. There
is a revival of what is simplistically called "supernaturalism",
God being sought and found in his intervention in the trivial
details of the individual's life, his power sufficient for
anything from a headache to a broken crankshaft. The decline
of the great preaching tradition is now explained by the too

little questioned maxim, "Conservative churches grow, liberal
churches decline", for the scholarly preaching and disciplined
evangelicalism of many of our fathers would now be dismissed
as "liberalism". Indeed, theology itself is suspect, whether
it originates from Alexandria, Augsburg or Geneva. Not surprisingly, a nation standing in the debris of its own history,
neither knowing it nor understanding it, has sired a generation
for whom history and, with it, the great theological enterprise,
are all but held in contempt.

Perhaps the slender theological supports of the liturgical
movement are beginning to buckle. The Reformation pattern of
word and sacrament is only dimly discerned in the self-indulgent
chaos that aspires to be worship of the holy, living God. It
is likely that little attention will be paid to the underlying
theological issues for one characteristic of many charismatic
churches is their numerical growth and their success where
others have failed. After years of decline such success is
seductive. Yet the merest glimpse at similar movements in the
past, of which the Welsh revivals are but one example, show
that a renewal that does not address itself to theology and
undergird experience with a strong concept of the church, ministry and sacraments, will not only fail to survive but will
leave the church weaker than it found it. It is the disturbing
failure to address these same questions that faces us in the
last movement to which we must give our attention.

The Church Growth Movement

The Church Growth Movement organizes the church for growth.
Using the insights of sociology and market research, it plots
courses of action that will lead to expansion. Goals are set
and success is looked for. Our present concern is with the
consequences this has for worship.

First, there is an overwhelming temptation to shape liturgy
to fit consumer needs. This often proves successful and the
theological questions are again set on one side. The topics
that occupied the minds of ministers during the liturgical
renewal are little understood, let alone debated. Worship as
shaped by what is owed to God and his glory, or worship that
embodies the tradition of the people of God has given way to
a style of worship that cultivates that sense of well-being
that the secular world has come to claim as a basic human
right.

Secondly, preaching is explicitly rejected as an effective
means of communicating the gospel. Preaching is not a factor
in church growth. This belief is now mathematically proven,
it is a statistical truism. Given our failure to carry through
our biblical and theological thinking on the meaning of eucharist, such a relegation of the ministry of the word can only
be viewed with alarm. The extent to which we have departed
from the :eformation tradition was evidenced at the 1980
Nottingham assembly where, from the public platform, ministers
were counselled to pay less attention to preaching and more to
congregational management on the grounds that "anyone can get

up and spout". From this astonishing description of preaching no one dissented.

Lastly, the Church Growth movement changes the nature of Christian ministry as a vocation to word and sacrament. Whereas this initially affects ministerial self-understanding such a view cannot but have repercussions in the worship of the church. Ministerial calling has been inextricably bound up with the liturgical offering of the church, week by week. Where calling is no longer understood in those terms a radical change has taken place. What seems a question of methodology has become a means of effecting a profound and disturbing shift in the theology of the church.

Not for the first time in the history of the church liturgy is the focal point of deeper theological issues. Earlier reference was made to numerical decline as the joker in the pack. That card has now appeared on the table, throwing into doubt and confusion the value of everything else that we hold in our hands. If truth is to be equated with success and error with failure, then a criterion has been introduced of which truth itself will be the first and greatest victim. We are no longer faced simply with questions of liturgical renewal. What is at issue is nothing less than our view of the Bible, the sacraments, our reformation tradition and the catholicity of the people of God. If preaching continues to be devalued, if the Lord's Supper is made marginal to the life of the church, if catholicity is rejected in favour of charismatic hedonism and fundamentalist authoritarianism then, whatever success may be ours numerically, it will have been purchased at the price of bankruptcy.

NOTES

1 *Baptist Magazine* 1868, p.102.

2 See C. H. Spurgeon, *Until He Come*, Prefatory Note.

3 John Clifford, *The True Use of the Lord's Supper* (1876), *The Ordinance of Jesus and the Sacraments of the Church* (1888).

MICHAEL WALKER

STILL AT THE CROSSROADS?

REVD J. H. SHAKESPEARE AND ECUMENISM

John Howard Shakespeare (1857-1928) was gripped by an ecumenical vision from the days of his Norwich ministry until his
death. Having put his hand to this plough, he never looked
back. His ecumenism was catholic and evangelical, strengthened by his distinctive interpretation of Baptist origins
which emphasised its Puritan rather than its Anabaptist roots,
and his fundamental commitment to Free Churchism as the vital
stepping stone towards a United Church in England. It was
evident in his deep commitment to the spirit of Edinburgh
1910 and his involvement from the first in the Faith and
Order Movement. But the event which convinced him it was
essential for the salvation of England was the trauma of the
First World War.

His convictions were summed up in his original and creative
treatment of Christian Unity in his most important book: *The
Churches at the Cross Roads*, published in 1918.[1] It closed
with these words:

> I passionately desire the goal of Church Unity, but
> it is an issue which I can leave with God. I have
> not the shadow of a doubt it will be reached, but
> He will appoint the instruments and determine the
> time. It is with bringing churches together as it
> is with the League of Nations to put an end to war.
> The difficulties are so many and so great that we
> feel it cannot be done. It is impossible - but the
> Church is always called to impossible tasks, and
> there is no other rational outlook for the world
> or the Church.[2]

It is this neglected aspect of Shakespeare's work that this
paper examines, for our present Baptist polity will be seriously misunderstood if the ecumenical vision with which
Shakespeare lived, as he restructured the Baptist Union, is
ignored.

J. C. Carlile's comments must always be treated with a
certain scepticism, but his view of Shakespeare is probably
accurate.

> Upon more than one occasion the Secretary of the Bap-
> tist Union came into sharp conflict with his brethren
> who could not understand his change of opinion. The
> fact is Shakespeare did not change his opinion; he
> had never believed in some positions assumed by the
> denomination to which he belonged, and he regarded
> all questions of organization as secondary.[3]

1.   THE   CHURCHES   AT   THE   CROSS   ROADS

This "study in church unity" glows with the passion of its
author for its theme. The book sold widely, was extensively
reviewed in the religious and secular press, and called forth
a torrent of correspondence in the various journals, much of
it negative, for months following.

Shakespeare began with a chapter on the old world and the
new, reflecting on the experience of those who, like himself,
had been born into the one and had come to live in the other.
Things which once gripped the passions of Christians had
shrunk to very small proportions. "The real religious questions of to-day have little or nothing to do with the sectarian conflicts of even twenty years ago".

In this new situation the resources of nervous energy were
nearly exhausted, but the Church which should be "a haven for
storm tossed humanity" was in fact failing its members. The
new situation revealed an "awakening of a conscience for social
service and of a resolve to secure a better chance for the
poor, the weak and the disinherited..." but "the doctrine of
laissez-faire, the emphasis laid upon the rights and liberty
of the individual, the calm acceptance even by Christian people
and philanthropists of the economic principles and results
which accumulated wealth in the hands of a few and sacrificed
the many, these things belong to that world order which is
passing away".[4]

The other new factor he noted was "the liberation of women
from the bonds of prejudice", viewing it as "the most hopeful
feature of our times. Only at its peril can the Church make
itself the last ditch of prejudice in this respect... In the
new world, women will enter upon hitherto untried paths, they
will assume added responsibilities and will advance in power,
efficiency, and self confidence; prejudices will disappear
and the Church will be compelled to accept the principle that
sex in itself can be no bar to position and service".[5]

Turning to discuss the place of the Church in the emerging
new world, he remarks that the days when "life itself, security, conduct, property, wars and foreign alliances turned on
the mysteries of religion and the articles of the Creed" have
gone, never to return. "The discussion of a sacrament or of
a form of Church polity will never again be a national event
of the first magnitude. The Church is not so much beset as
disregarded".[6]

Shakespeare noted seven points by which the Church must
justify itself and act in this new world:

(1)   The "supreme function of the Church is to know God,
and to makes its idea of God operative in human lives".[7]
The theology of a book like H. G. Wells's *God the Invisible
King* was doomed to failure because it was fashioned out of
the author's imagination.

> The Church cannot maintain itself on anything less
> actual than the Incarnation, the Cross and the Re-
> surrection. The relation of God to a world in which

sin is an awful reality can never be adequately expressed by genial and tolerant kindliness... the
Church must know God with depths of humility and
penitence, it must know Him for itself, not by tradition or in a creed, but with a vital, penetrating
knowledge which dominates its worship, thought and
activity, if it is to make its distinctive impression
upon the world. [8]

(ii)   The true objective of the Church is to establish the
Kingdom of God in the world.   The Church as we know it is insufficient for that task.   The present recrudescence of paganism and denial of the Christian ethic makes the Church's
task harder.   Can there be a rebirth of the Church?, questioned Shakespeare.

The insistence has been too much upon orthodoxy of
creed. Opinions and creeds have their rightful place,
but the emphasis of Christ's teaching was upon love
and forgiveness and mercy... The Church, if it is
to have a distinctive morality, must get back to
simplicity. [9]

(iii)   The Church in the new world must be ready to risk
something.

It cannot appeal to a time which has risked everything
in the storm of war unless it is itself heroic, going
out on great adventures, attempting impossible tasks,
and facing difficult enterprises. [10]

(iv)   The Church must understand the attitude and temper
of its own time, looking through its eyes, speaking
its vocabulary, and wearing its garb. [11]

The re-statement of the Church's faith must take into account
the rational, scientific and social principles upon which the
progress and hope of the new world is being built.   An obscur-
antist Church will fail modern man totally.

It is simply disastrous when men, wrapped in grave-
clothes of dead controversies, utter battle cries
which have lost all their power. [12]

(v)   The Church must take its part in solving the "ills
of society".   The individualism which has been the mainspring
of the tremendous growth in economic wealth has pressed hard
upon the poor.

The contribution of the Church as a Church will not be
by way of programme, or by linking itself to any party
in the State, but by infusing the spirit of Christ into
human affairs, by insisting there are no rights without
correlative duties, and that the accumulation of wealth
without any care as to how it is obtained and for merely selfish use and ease, is a sin against God and man. [13]

(vi)   "The Church must transcend Nationalism".[14]   Indeed,
the situation demands a very different kind of Church from
anything the world has yet seen, if it is to prevent or re-
strain war.   "It must be a Church in communion in its different parts, for a divided Church cannot speak effectively to
a divided world".[15]

(vii)   The Church must be ready to step out into this new
world, on to the offensive for the Kingdom of God.   We cannot
"imagine what the Church of our day would be like if it had
no 'foreign legion', but only crouched within its own confines,
selfishly seeking to keep its soul alive".[16]

Shakespeare painted a church re-born in bold strokes, but
he has to admit that though the Christian religion is about
love and fellowship, "Organized Christianity does not strike
the world in quite this way".[17]   It is split into denominations,
which by their very names place that which is divisive to the
forefront, witnessing, not to Christ, but to historical controversy.

It is his contention that, despite this, Evangelical Free
Churches are *not* legion, and share a common origin, emphasis
and conviction.

> First, that Church is composed of those who have been
> born again, and that its membership is not co-extensive
> with the nation or secured by the sacraments of baptism
> and confirmation; second, that the internal life of the
> Church is a spiritual fellowship, totally different
> from the secular relation of parishioners; and, thirdly,
> that the authority of the Church is vested under Christ
> Himself in the people of God as distinct from govern-
> ment by a clerical or sacerdotal hierarchy...   The
> essential oneness of the Evangelical Free Churches may
> be carried a little further.   To a greater or lesser
> extent, they trust the people.[18]

Shakespeare concludes his chapter: "The grand passion for
a Church truly holy, truly Catholic; a Church which can, if
needs be, override its past... is the passion which should
inflame and enlarge our hearts".[19]The heart of Shakespeare's
critique of the churches is the assessment of denominationalism - its gains and losses.   It is important to understand
that he believed separation was the essence of denominationalism.

> A denomination begins when a number of adherents set
> up a corporate Church fellowship on the basis of cer-
> tain tenets or practices which they regard as suffi-
> ciently important to break up one fellowship and to
> constitute another.   The ground of the separation is
> that the conscience of the adherent does not permit
> him to be a member of a Church which does not avow a
> certain tenet, or maintain a certain order, or observe
> a certain rite.[20]

The gains of denominationalism were three. (i) It emphasised truths or certain aspects of truth which had been obscured, forgotten or denied. There must be a considerable
debt of gratitude due to those who "struggled desperately in
the darkness to keep a foothold upon the unseen and eternal".[21]
(ii) There had been a practical witness to the devout and
unworldly life, distinctive in Puritanism and Methodism in the
past. "The strength of the Free Churches has always been in
their piety. They have had nothing else to offer".[22]
(iii) The distinctive ordering of Free Churches, in the government of themselves, their worship and witness, was a contribution which could be rightly made to "the common enrichment of the united Church".[23]

The losses of denominationalism were more starkly presented
and at much greater length. Proposing a parallel between
Pharisaism and Puritanism, Shakespeare warned the Free Churches
they "may be holding to a shell or to a form from which the
spirit has departed... so far as English religious life is
concerned, the era of division has spent its force and lost
its moral appeal".[24]

The losses were clear in denominational returns, which revealed a decline of 100,000 Free Church members between 1906
and 1916. The losses were not the result of stricter discipline, nor were they accompanied by an increase of prayer and
spirituality - "Probably the very reverse is nearer the
truth". Failure to arrest this decline now would result in
the denominations "slowly bleeding to death".[25]

The existing division into denominations diverts the ener-
gies of Church and minister from the spiritual to the material,
often converting the Church into a business concern.

Denominationalism is making no progress because it makes
no appeal to the conscience and intellect of the best elements
in the nation who are outside the churches. "They see that
the real issue of our time is not in the things that divide
the churches but in the war they wage together against the
forces of evil".[26] Shakespeare tells, at some length, of a
colleague who lost two sons in the War, and who commented to
him: "the sects as such can do nothing at all. The things
they stand for in their divisions may be true and good as far
as they go, but they do not matter. They simply and finally
do not matter in this tragic hour".[27]

Most serious of all is the fact that denominationalism is
failing because the members no longer believe in it.

> The plain fact is that the vast tree of sectarian
> divisions is rapidly becoming hollow: it is propped
> up by iron bands of trust deeds and funds and by
> that conservatism which is so beautiful and touching
> when it confines itself to 'ivy mantled towers' and
> 'moping owls'. One day, in a general storm, the
> hollow tree will come down with a crash... Advancing
> with the inevitableness of the dawn and the energy of
> springtime is the growing conviction that the actual
> differences are not a sufficient ground for separation.[28]

In the light of such things, how could Shakespeare have spent all his days as Secretary of the Baptist Union, in fact strengthening denominationalism?

> No one could ever regard me as an indifferent Baptist. I plan and toil for the Church of my own faith, that when the grand festival of union comes she may be led to the altar in radiant beauty, a bride anyone may be proud to have... Yet... the days of denominationalism are numbered. There is nothing more pathetic or useless, in this world, than clinging to dead issues, worn-out methods and antiquated programmes.[29]

The tragedy of denominationalism was seen in the inability of the Free Churches to mount a mission to the nation like that of the Anglican National Mission of Repentance and Hope. The supply, training, spheres and ideals of the ministry were all hampered by the denominationalism which encouraged sectarian antagonism in every village and town. But most serious of all was the problem of the "overlapping" of the Free Churches' religious forces.

> The chief argument for Free Church unity has always consisted for me in the ideal purpose and spirit of the Church itself, but I must frankly confess that my audiences everywhere have been chiefly moved by the folly and shame of overlapping.[30]

Shakespeare's final challenge was set within a firm Biblical precedent.

> Have [they] realized that [they] may be called by God to seem to turn [their] back upon [their] past? The Jew of the Apostolic Church found it hard to forsake Abraham and Moses and the oracles of God... on the way to Damascus obedience to the heavenly vision may be to heal the wounds and end the separation which [their] fathers made... To cling to great names and institutions and vested interests and formulae is to forswear the control of the living God for that of the dead hand... The Free Churches have reached a stage in the religious life of this country when, if they are simply a denomination and not a united church, they are doomed.[31]

Shakespeare now turned to his own understanding of Church unity. He states it positively and clearly.

> By the unity of the Church we mean that the different parts of the one body work together in complete harmony of means and end without any collision or frustration of the life force, each organ fulfilling its function and answering to its own type.[32]

Church unity is NOT co-operation in social service, moral campaigns and civic action - it "can only be 'fully realized through community of worship, faith and order'".[33] Neither is it identical with inter-communion, though it cannot exist without it. Church unity is in essence different from uniformity, and can never be a mechanical device engineered by clever scheming and planning.

> Uniformity is un-catholic. The Catholic Church has
> in all ages recognized diversities of faith, rites,
> ceremonies and operations. The vital sources within
> the Church have broken out into a rich fertility,
> Catholicism has never required a pale and colourless
> identity of ritual or doctrine.[34]

Shakespeare accepted that Macaulay had a point when he suggested that "uniformity" had been a fatal mistake of Anglicanism at the Reformation, and that if Anglicanism had understood Catholicism it would have made the nonconformists its
champions.

> At Rome the Countess of Huntingdon would have a place
> in the calendar as St Selina; and Mrs Fry would be
> foundress and first Superior of the Blessed Order of
> Sisters of the Gaols.[35]

"Unity is not the only word, yet it is the great and impressive word of our time",[36] claimed Shakespeare, and the
Churches have fallen short of the New Testament ideal. The
churches must face the new age by closing their ranks, since
unrelieved denominationalism will involve inevitable and increasing loss. "The churches must seek unity and establish
closer relations that religion itself may be saved".[37]

Shakespeare rehearsed the steps taken since his presidential challenge to Free Church unity issued in 1916 to the
National Free Church Council. The way of corporate union,
though urged by Shakespeare, was not taken, and instead the
way of Federation was being pursued. Federation was not a
final goal, nor an ideal solution, but an intermediate step
aimed at "reconciliation of autonomy with co-operation, liberty with order, and unity with diversity".[38] The federal idea
would depend upon a clear understanding of the Christian faith,
and Shakespeare welcomed the Declaratory Statement which had
been drawn up as "catholic, evangelical and positive".[39]

Federation would mean one united Free Church in each village of England. He looked for the creation of Free Church
parishes, countrywide, and urged the appointment of "Home
Mission Superintendents to go with apostolic zeal through the
land to cheer, to advise and to perfect in every parish the
organization for bringing religion to the homes of the people".[40]
Ministerial training would be shared by all Free Churches in
a university setting, rather than in "the narrow grooves and
the denominational atmosphere of the theological seminary".[41]
The Edinburgh Conference "comity of mission" plans had shown
the way. "As the early Church confronted Paganism and resisted it even unto blood, so we may have to set ourselves in
union for the defence of the Faith".[42]

The Federal Council is not the Free Church Council under
another name. The Federal Council will be exclusively representative, each member appointed by and responsible to his
own denomination. The Federal Council will deal with matters

of Faith, ministry, united evangelism, and the deployment of
forces to remove overlapping. There is no danger of uniformity in the Federal Council since only an insane person would
"think there would be any real danger of a dead and insipid
uniformity in a union which included Baptists and Presbyterians, Wesleyans and Congregationalists".[43]

There were problems to be faced when joining the Connex-
ional and Congregational orders of administration; and persuading village churches to catch a vision of "the Catholic
Church" was no easy task; but the issue would be finally resolved by the leadership given in each denomination in the
coming generation.

Shakespeare did not shirk the issue of what such a federal
unity might mean for future negotiations about reunion with
the Church of England. However, he was convinced that the
aim must be to bring to "an end that tremendous cleavage in
the religious life of this realm which followed the Act of
Uniformity in 1662".[44]

The way out of the "maze" was by a recognition that in 1662
the situation was one of intolerance, and their idea of peace
was an unconditional surrender. The position now is that
both Catholic and Puritan have felt the shame and sorrow of
division, "the temper of our time is eirenical... Catholic
and Puritan are complementary to each other... need each other
for full-orbed faith and order".[45]

> Catholicism has produced its saints, but never, I
> think, a saintly Church or a saintly nation...
> Puritanism also has produced saints, and I think,
> once a saintly Church, but never a saintly nation.
> To-day it seems to me that neither Catholic nor
> Puritan produces a saintly Church or a saintly
> nation. Catholicism stands for authority, Puri-
> tanism for freedom; Catholicism for the sacrament,
> Puritanism for the Word; Catholicism for the Church,
> Puritanism for the Gospel; Catholicism for the
> cloister, Puritanism for the open air. But they
> come together in this, that they both regard re-
> ligion as the chief and real business of life.[46]

Shakespeare grasped the nettle of episcopacy. "It is no
use concealing my conviction that reunion will never come to
pass except upon the basis of episcopacy. I did not think
so once, but that was simply because I did not understand it".[47]

He refers to the evidence of "episcopal, presbyteral, and
congregational" forms of church government in the New Testament. However, "when we get to close quarters", Free Churchmen learn that unity with Anglicans must mean some kind of
episcopal system, since "the Church of England is not united
in a theory of episcopacy, but in episcopacy itself as a form
of government".[48]

Shakespeare described the changes which had taken place in
himself by saying that over the years, "I seem to myself to
have travelled into a new country".[49] He was correct. He
did not suddenly arrive at these conclusions, they were within

him from the beginning, perhaps more than he himself realised.

2. WHAT PRECEDED THE BOOK?

In the final chapter Shakespeare saw himself at the beginning of his ministry as "a Baptist of the Baptists and a dis-
senter of the dissenters". The two events he recalled concerning his ministry in Norwich were contrasting - the success
of a united Free Church Mission led, at Shakespeare's youthful
invitation, by Hugh Price Hughes; and the coolness of his reception at the Anglican Church Congress, when he spoke for
Norwich Nonconformists a message of welcome. It "left on my
mind at the time the impression that it was best for us to go
our own way and not to attempt these unwelcome attentions...
the gulf was too wide for us even to shake hands across it".[50]
But that was *not* how he summed up his years in Norwich when
he replied to the address of the St Mary's Church Secretary
on 17th October 1898, just before he took up his position as
General Secretary of the Baptist Union.

> I am conscious that I have changed in many directions.
> I was brought up in a very severe and strict school of
> of ecclesiastical thought. I probably attached too
> much importance to the questions which divide Chris-
> tians from each other. I was fond of controversy...
> But I have learned to say with an intenser meaning,
> "grace, mercy and peace be with all who love our Lord
> Jesus Christ in sincerity and truth". I hold my own
> convictions as strongly as ever, but I trust that I
> respect the sincere convictions of other Christians
> more than I did... I have learnt that it is not my
> work to disparage or fight against any other church,
> but I desire to stand side by side with all other
> followers of Christ in winning the world to God.[51]

What did Shakespeare actually say at the welcome to the
Church Congress in 1895?

> We recall with gratitude our own debt to you, for the
> thoughts of your great preachers and teachers have
> entered like iron into our blood, and have coloured
> and inspired our whole ministry. It is your inalien-
> able glory that generation after generation you have
> maintained the unfailing use of common prayer and the
> regular reading of the Word of God. In a secular age
> you have offered a persistent witness to the best
> things... You have had the sagacity to perceive and
> the energy to grapple with the changed conditions of
> population and the rapid growth of towns and there
> is no suburb in England in which the spire does not
> rise as the symbol of your awakened zeal and profound
> statesmanship...

> The problem of the continued separation between the
> Anglican Church and Nonconformity was never more
> living and immediate than it is at present...

> We cannot doubt that a new spirit is abroad, a weariness

of strife and turmoil, and of yearning for Christian
fellowship... The spirit of peace comes upon [institu-
tions and churches too] not an indifference to the
truth, but a very solemn feeling that division must
mean mutual loss... I for one am not prepared to admit
that our differences are final and hopeless.

Whenever proposals for reunion are made, a crowd of
prejudiced and heated partisans at once fasten on some
minor point, and nail their colours to what they call
the mast, but which is only one of the ship's spars.
They divert attention from that which is fundamental.

It may be, dear and honoured brethren in Christ... that
as you read you loyalty to Christ you cannot acknowledge
our ministry and our Church life. If this be so the
question of organic reunion is indeed an insoluble one.
Much as we covet your fellowship, we must elect to stand
by our spiritual ancestry... Perhaps we are to find that
the "dearest bond of love" is not "like to like, but
like in difference"...

Whether we are conscious of it or no, the realities
which unite us infinitely transcend our differences,
grave and serious as they are, since we have one hope
of our calling, one Lord, one faith, one baptism, one
God and Father of all... [52]

Certainly Shakespeare did not blur the issue, but his own
desire for unity is evident - a conviction endorsed by an un-
solicited testimony from the Rev. C. R. Lloyd Engstrom, Rector
of St Mildred, Bread Street, London, Secretary of the Christian Evidence Society, who was given hospitality by the Shake-
speares during the Congress. In his address to the Congress
he noted:

I happen as a member of this Church Congress, to have
had a real privilege. I have been entertained with
the greatest hospitality and kindness conceivable by
himself and his wife - both hitherto unknown to me even
by name - in the house of a leading Baptist minister in
Norwich, the Rev. J. H. Shakespeare. I only wish all
of you could have had the opportunity of hearing what
has passed between us in conversation on the points
which separate Baptists from Churchmen, and of knowing
how lovingly he regards the Church of England, not
only when speaking to me, but when speaking to his
Nonconformist brethren, and I am sure you would have
been drawn towards men like Mr Shakespeare. [53]

A year later, it is no surprise to learn that Shakespeare was
addressing the Evangelical Anglican Fraternal, the Norwich
Clerical Society. Though he did not hold the connection of
Church and State to be intrinsically wrong, reported the
Christian World , he did believe that reunion would be has-
tened by removing the Church of England from State interference. [54]

It has been noted by many that Dr Dale of Birmingham encouraged Shakespeare in 1893 to accept a call from Hagley
Road Baptist Church, Birmingham. What is not so widely known
is why he refused it. He notified the Church of the invitation on 13th February 1893, and at a special Church Meeting
on 20th February indicated that he "would be largely influenced by the opinion of the Church and congregation". The
thrust of Dale's letter was that there was "no leading man"
among Birmingham Baptists, and that Shakespeare would be better able to carry on the Church extension programme which he
had been advocating. The St Mary's members "assured him of
their unbroken confidence and affection and of the very deep
regret which the thought of him possibly leaving them for
another sphere has caused...". The following letter was read
to the Meeting from the Secretary of the Congregational
Churches of Norwich, J. Jewin:

> At a meeting of the Pastors and Deacons of the Con-
> gregational Churches in this city held at the Old
> Meeting House, on Friday evening, I was requested as
> chairman of that meeting to write expressing our deep
> sympathy with the Church at St Mary's in the present
> important crisis, a crisis which affects not only
> your Church but the position of Nonconformity in this
> city - Trusting the Great Head of the Church may guide
> your deliberations tonight and bring them to a wise
> and satisfactory issue.

On 5th March 1893 the Pastor indicated to the Church his
intention to stay in Norwich, and noted not only what the
Church Meeting had said, but also "the representations made
to him as to the needs of nonconformity in Norwich and Norfolk".[55]

Further evidence of Shakespeare's broader sympathies are
revealed in his attachment to the Free Church Council movement which sprang from the "grass-roots" Nonconformist scene
of his day. It arose out of the Nonconformist engagement
with social questions. Locally it concerned missions, temperance demonstrations, lectures on nonconformist principles,
and school board elections. Shakespeare, just two years into
his pastorate, preached *An Election Sermon - The Duty of
Christian Men in the present Political Crisis* on 15th November 1885, which he recognised would "certainly incur the dis-
pleasure of some who are present and many who are absent".
He claimed:

> It is a cardinal principle with me that, if religion
> is to be worth anything, it must not be the religion
> merely of the cloister or of speculative thought,
> but in actual contact with an actual world... we
> should make more progress if theologians would tell
> us more of God's message to a work-a-day world...
> The Christian has a political as well as a religious
> duty to discharge, but in it he will be animated,
> controlled, and decided by his duty towards God...[56]

Though by 1918 Shakespeare wrote that he felt the Free
Church Council had been "driven in upon itself, become more
and more political... and perhaps has fulfilled its mission",[57]
he still maintained close links with Lloyd George.   At the
"coupon election" he was an active supporter, being involved
at Downing Street when the election manifesto was drawn.
T. Wilson claims: "Whereas by 1918 prominent divines like
Maud Royden were moving over to the Labour Party, others like
Dr Shakespeare had followed Lloyd George in to Conservative
company".[58]   Certainly Shakespeare supported Lloyd George in
the columns of the *Baptist Times*, and was reprimanded for this
by the Yorkshire Baptist Association.[59]   The Yorkshire resolution was published, and the editorial comment was incisive.

> We make no apology for our political notes.   We have
> never attempted to write vapid nothings.   We are sup-
> porters of Mr Lloyd George and the coalition and no
> one imagines that what we write is in an official
> capacity.   Nevertheless we firmly believe that our
> official view is that of the immense majority of the
> Baptist denomination.[60]

Perhaps it was his personal friendship with Lloyd George
which accounted for Shakespeare's growing frustration with
the Free Church Council, politically.   Certainly he believed
that his advocacy of Christian unity through the Free Church
Council had been as a voice crying in the wilderness.   In 1916,
opening his presidential address to the Free Church Council,
he said:

> For six years I have been preaching from the same text.
> You have maintained for the most part a discreet and
> sometimes a perplexed silence.   I have no more know-
> ledge of what you really think than the preacher has
> of what is passing through the minds of his congrega-
> tion while he speaks to them from the pulpit.   I ven-
> ture to think that the moment is urgent and that it
> is high time to abandon your detached and judicial
> attitude, to come to some decision and let us know
> where you are.[61]

As early as 1888 Shakespeare was taking holidays at Grindelwald, almost certainly sharing in the holiday parties arranged
by Henry Lunn which were composed of representatives of various
churches.   Knowledge of this comes from the Deacons' Minutes
at St Mary's, for 17th August that year, where it is agreed
that £55 be credited to the Pastor's account, which will enable
him to take the rest and change which he was ordered, "free
from all pecuniary anxiety".

In his letter, also recorded under that date, Shakespeare
wrote:

> And now as to myself - as you know at Grindelwald I
> could not sleep or eat and suffered from a constant
> headache - But at Murren I was in quite a different
> atmosphere and the last week made almost a new man of
> me - progressing every day since the change and am
> now almost free from headache - and have become quite

stout. The hotel is on the high ground and the
scenery round is much more open here than at
Grindelwald.

The Congregational and Baptist Unions had had a joint Assembly in 1886, and heard with enthusiasm a paper deprecating
competition. In 1889, under the heading "Nonconformist Church
Extension", Shakespeare reported to his deacons a proposal
that Congregationalists and Baptists should unite in a fund
to erect new chapels in Norwich. "The idea being to build
two union places of worship, one to have a Baptist and the
other to have a Paedo Baptist minister". A conference was
held at Princes Street, Norwich on 3rd January 1890. By 11th
March 1890 it had to be reported that the scheme had fallen
through, but that George White and H. P. Gould would represent the diaconate on a committee to consider a further scheme.[62]

It was in 1906 that the further development of this kind
of thinking was published by Shakespeare in a book which
formed part of a twelve volume series called "Eras of Nonconformity", edited by C. Silvester Horne. It was entitled
Baptist and Congregational Pioneers,[63] and dedicated to William Goodman, Shakespeare's father-in-law, who "throughout a
long life, has exemplified the best traditions of Free Churchism".

The main importance of the era he was to describe, wrote
Shakespeare in the Preface, was "the historic explanation
which it supplies as to the origin and nature of the existing
cleavage in English religious and ecclesiastical life". In
this task we may assume that his brother-in-law, W. T. Whitley,
the founder of the Baptist Historical Society in 1908, was a
valuable ally. Shakespeare makes it clear that "it is entirely unhistorical and misleading to confuse the English
Baptists with Anabaptists... they were marked off from each
other by differences of origin, doctrine, social and political
ideas".[64] Baptist pioneers, were for Shakespeare, the "English Separatists, congregational in church polity and anti-
paedo-Baptist in practice, who gave rise to indigenous churches in this country".[65]

We are not surprised to find that John Smyth is for Shakespeare the founder of modern Baptist churches, who formed Baptist principles in his "noble and historic confession", sepa-
rating "like dross from gold" those "elements of Anabaptism
which would never have communicated themselves to the practical English mind".[66]

Among the Congregationalists we find that Shakespeare
honoured John Robinson's "peaceful church" at Leyden. To
Robinson, he noted, "Spirit was infinitely more... than form"
and what offended Robinson most were those who were "stiff
and rigid in matters of outward order and inveigh against the
evils of others".[67]

One other sentence is worth noting: "It is vital to note
that the Puritans were within the Church of England. Many of
them not only accepted episcopacy but believed in it".[68]
This is a theme to which he returned much later, when facing

the prospect of reunion with the Anglicans.

In 1906 Shakespeare had laid before a committee of the
Baptist Union four propositions:

> (i) That the New Testament conception of the visible
> church admits of there being a common church in one
> town or district, consisting of all the believers in
> that town or district.

> (ii) That the New Testament conception admits of a
> number of companies of believers, while forming part
> of a common Church, yet meeting separately for worship
> and service.

> (iii) That there should be one eldership for the com-
> mon church, in which each company of believers is re-
> presented.

> (iv) That the common church should appoint the pastors
> and assign to them the services they shall respectively
> render. [69]

At the autumn Assembly of the Baptist Union two papers were
given. Dr Henderson spoke on the "interpretation of Congregationalism as resting on the authority of Scripture". Dr Robinson's paper was on "Congregationalism as illustrated in the
sub-apostolic period". Both papers concluded with support for
a dictum of Shakespeare's that "Congregationalism interpreted
as Independency was not only unequal to the solution of the
problems which were before the denomination but was unscrip-
tural". [70]

Shakespeare's attempt to mould Free Church opinion towards
a united Free Church in England began seriously in 1910. In
an address to the Council he suggested "a United Board to
supervise a redistribution of Free Church resources and to
undertake a wide social and evangelistic service". Once,
claimed Shakespeare, the greatest contribution the Free Churches were able to make to the Kingdom of God had been division
and separation, but the hour had come when a United Free Church,
purged of inessentials and rivalry, could strike a mighty blow
for the salvation of England. Shakespeare developed his proposals in the *Christian World* and other great leaders like
Charles Brown, Silvester Horne, Scott Lidgett, J. H. Jowett
and Peter Forsyth quickly rallied to his side. [71]

The following year an inquiry was established as a necessary
preliminary to a successful outcome. In proposing this Shakespeare said their concern should not be "a mechanical but a
living union... We must convince little communities which are
so engrossed with denominational cares and local struggles
that there is a Holy Catholic Church". [72] "Free Churchism is
here... and it has a destiny if it keeps in touch with the
living present. It appeals to half the religious forces of
the nation...". Free Churchism and Anglicanism should com-
plement each other, "rejoicing in each other's service to the
Kingdom of God... To do that effectively means putting the
Free Church house in order. The task is to save Free Churchism

and to save the people. In a sense these two are one. The
only way in which a Church can save is by losing itself".[73]
The Free Churches can no longer stand quite where their forefathers did. "We have to make our own witness: we have to
strike the note of unity and urge that many of our divisions
have fulfilled their purpose... Brethren, we of the Free
Churches must go forward with God... facing the new ways in
his strength".[74]

   In 1916 Shakespeare came to the chair of the Free Church
Council, and having "always felt that it was the business of
a leader to lead", he rehearsed before them the main arguments
which later formed the first part of *The Churches at the Cross
Roads*, though with no suggestion of reunion with the Church
of England, which dominated the later part of that book.

> We have reached a stage in the religious life of this
> country, when, if we are simply denominations and not
> a united Church, we are doomed. The principle of
> division has spent its force and the era of union
> must begin...

Having outlined his proposals for Federation and the arguments
for them, he asked:

> I wonder whether these arguments make the same impres-
> sion on your mind as they do on mine? Is it not time
> that the leaders began to lead and that you gave up
> your discreet and ambiguous silence?... I would beseech
> you not to face a great issue with sterile platitudes
> and trivial arguments... To-day I rear upon the field
> the standard of the United Free Church of England.
> Let all who are ready to do battle for the cause gather
> beneath its folds.[75]

Shakespeare's address was printed in tens of thousands and
widely sold among the Free Churches. He himself toured the
constituency, personally visiting as many as forty Federations
in the year as well as numerous local Councils and churches.
The results of this were noted in the Free Church Year Book
of 1917:

> There cannot be the least question that the people
> are with the movement. They are convinced and they
> are impatient for action. They are tired of inertia
> and delay. This verdict has come from the members
> of every denomination.[76]

Shakespeare also toured the Free Church denominational
assemblies and annual gatherings to gain the support there
for his proposals. He was entirely successful and each denomination appointed representatives to the Conference held
at Mansfield College, in 1916, and at Cambridge in 1917. The
Faith, ministry, evangelism, and the nature of Federation were
all considered. The primary plan was for a Federal Council
constituted of officially authorized delegates endorsed by the
denominations. The Statement of Faith, drafted by Dr Carnegie
Simpson, was not an exhaustive creed but a public and corporate testimony.

The Federation proposals came before the Baptist Union
Assembly in 1918. Shakespeare was forceful and frank in asking
Baptist acceptance of the plan.

> This tender little plant lifts its head timidly above
> the ground after the long winter of sectarianism but
> it has in it the promise of spring. It says, "Do not
> mistake me. I am not organic union. I am only a
> Federation. Do not stamp on me or crush me. Nurture
> me..." Ours is the first denominational assembly to
> consider the Report. It is unthinkable that Baptists
> should wreck the movement or even look at it with dis-
> trust and hesitation.[77]

Baptists did not crush it, immediately, and other denominational Assemblies accepted it, though the Wesleyans delayed
for a year. The Federal Council of Evangelical Free Churches
was born in October 1919, merging with the National Free Church
Council in 1940.

3. WHAT FOLLOWED THE BOOK'S PUBLICATION?

The publication of *The Churches at the Crossroads* made it
abundantly clear that Shakespeare had moved far beyond his
address to the Free Church Council in 1916. In fact, the
evidence is that as early as 1913-14 he had begun to reassess
his attitude to Anglicanism. He had welcomed the Edinburgh
Conference in 1910, and in particular had become involved with
the Faith and Order movement which flowed from it. He was one
of a group of Free Church leaders who actively encouraged a
continuing encounter between the Church of England and the
Free Churches in April 1914. Two interim Reports were produced,
titled *Towards Christian Unity*, the first appearing in February
1916, and the other in March 1918.

The Secretary of the Faith and Order meeting was the Rev.
Tissington Tatlow. On 7th May 1915, Shakespeare wrote a long
letter to him, expressing his own convictions at that date:
"The present division between the Established and Nonconformist
Churches is a grave scandal in the religious life of this country. It is worthwhile making an effort to bridge the chasm
which through many blunders came about in 1662". Now that the
matter of Orders and Sacraments are before the group, and they
have already "as to the Faith substantial agreement", Shakespeare is eager "to establish as much agreement as we can in
essentials".

> Ought we not to consider very carefully whether too
> great importance has not been attached to the Form,
> and whether the Form can be so vital if
> (a) the darkest ages of Church History have been those
> in which the Form was practically undisputed
> (b) many of the greatest saints of the Church, many
> good men, have only been able to save their souls and
> preserve religion by abandoning the Form and
> (c) through the churches which have not the same Form
> there flows to members the same Divine Life.

Does Church unity require that there should be only
one possible Form for a valid ministry or sacrament?
The branches of the Church do recognize many variations
in Form, for example, Roman, Anglican, Eastern Nes-
torian.   Is Anglicanism not prepared to recognize any
variation which would bring Free Churchism into communion?

If the historic Episcopate is vital to the Church and
the Sacraments, is it conceivable
(a) that such a requirement should not be found with
any clearness in the New Testament; that it is indeed
so hidden that a sincere theologian like Dr Forsyth
should write: "The form of polity is indifferent for
faith";
(b) that the maintenance of the succession cannot be
proved... for lack of documents
(c) so far as we have the evidence in the second century at least one Church, Alexandria, did not possess
the historic Episcopate in the sense of Dr Robinson
(d) to attach such value to Form seems contrary to
the spirit of Christ and of St Paul...

The question is rather whether Anglicanism is prepared for the purposes of Communion to acknowledge a
ministry which derives its validity from Christ
through the people of God.   Free Churchism can claim
such a ministry.   We have an undoubted succession in
the call to the ministry by the succession of believers.

Finally, I suggest that in this matter the Church of
England represents history - we stand in this argument
for Christian experience.   Is it possible that we
could agree to require as a minimum for the purposes
of Communion only what can be derived from the New
Testament?...[78]

By the time Shakespeare wrote his book, he knew that episcopacy, in some form, was crucial for Anglicanism.

It is no use concealing my conviction that reunion
will never come to pass except upon the basis of
episcopacy.   I did not think so once, but that was
simply because I did not understand it.[79]

T. R. Glover led the denominational opposition to Shakespeare.   In a resolution which was carried at the Assembly
on 29th April 1919, he noted that:

If the price of Ecclesiastical Reunion be the acceptance of episcopacy, in its historical sense or in
some non-historical sense, with the implied necessity
of regularizing our ministry by episcopal ordination
or re-ordination, the Baptists of this country...
elect to stand by the Priesthood of all believers
and God's right to call and consecrate whom He will
and how He will.[80]

Wheeler Robinson gave *The Churches at the Cross Roads* a
cautious review in the *Baptist Times*, not least because he
was becoming increasingly convinced that organic union was
not the way forward, and that "fellowship at the Lord's Table
must precede, not follow, attempts to unite episcopal and non-
episcopal churches".[81]

Glover's 1919 Baptist Union resolution was the result of
an editorial by Robertson Nicoll, in the *British Weekly* on 5th
December 1918, titled "Mr Shakespeare at the Crossroads". It
was a stinging personal attack upon Shakespeare.

> Two Archbishops and he signed the last interim report
> issued by the Committee which advocated reunion between
> Anglicans and Nonconformists upon the basis of the
> "acceptance of the fact of Episcopacy". He implies
> unmistakably that Free Church ministers will have to
> submit to episcopal re-ordination. We cannot hope to
> achieve reunion in any other way - but Mr Shakespeare
> considers it well worth the price. He appears to have
> recognised, somewhat late in life, the fascination of
> the Anglican communion; he feels the spell of its piety,
> its culture, its venerable liturgy... Moreover he is
> genuinely moved by the new impulse towards unity which
> is re-fashioning all our parties and politics. And he
> is terribly afraid of dropping out of what he takes to
> be the current stream or tendency. Motives like these
> lead him on to assume that Church Unity is a duty so
> imperious that Christian men ought to give up almost
> anything to attain it...

> It is time to speak plainly about this business in
> which Mr Shakespeare is one of the main protagonists.
> It has gone quite far enough while people were too pre-
> occupied with the War to pay attention to private en-
> claves of ecclesiastics in Oxford.

> We challenge Mr Shakespeare to put the straightforward
> issue before the Baptist Union next May and to ask the
> rank and file of delegates to say whether their Secre-
> tary is representing them or vitally misrepresenting
> them.

> Five and twenty years ago we ardently defended the
> Baptist Union when Mr Spurgeon denounced its members
> as being on the "down grade". We are confident that
> they are not on the "down grade" today. Mr Shakespeare
> will find no followers along the steep gradient down
> which he is pointing them. But one thing we cannot
> help regretting: we do wish it were possible to hear
> Mr Spurgeon on Mr Shakespeare.

The whole matter entered a new phase when it was learned
that the Anglicans were seeking official conversations about
more comprehensive church relations in England. The Lambeth
"Appeal to All Christian People" ushered in a new stage in
Anglican-Free Church relationships and led to a series of
conversations between the representatives of the Federal Coun-

cil, of which Shakespeare was the first President, and a
group of Anglicans nominated by the Archbishop of Canterbury.

Shakespeare had told the Free Church Council that he believed leaders should lead. He told the Baptist Assembly,
when he spoke to Glover's resolution in April 1919, that "in
leading this movement I have no intention of stampeding the
Baptist denomination or doing anything dishonourable" and he
concluded "I am not at the crossroads. I have chosen my path
and I shall follow it".[82]

Shakespeare commented to Archbishop Lang that the "Appeal"
is "the finger of God".[83]   T. R. Glover wrote a series of
brillian articles for the *British Weekly* which Heffer's published under the title *The Free Churches and Reunion*, commended in a preface by the veteran John Clifford who, after long
silence, finally declared himself against the Secretary of
the Union.

Shakespeare used his influence to have the Archbishop of
York, Cosmo Gordon Lang, to address the Baptist Union Assembly
on the "Appeal" in 1921.   Shakespeare was so thrilled with the
event that he wrote afterwards to Lang: "Your address was so
persuasive that I said that if someone had risen and moved
that we accept episcopal ordination, it could have been carried.
I think perhaps this is an exaggeration, but something very
near it would have been reached".

Lang's reaction was much more down to earth.   After his
addresses to the Baptist and Presbyterian Assemblies, he commented: "In both cases the reception was very cordial to me
personally, but I do not think these good people have any real
care about a visible Church at all.   I am afraid they are still
content if only they can preach at St Paul's and communicate
at our altars".[84]

In 1922 Shakespeare contributed a chapter to a volume of
essays edited by James Marchant, *The Coming Renaissance*.[85]
Under the heading "Where the Renaissance must begin", Shakespeare spoke about the reaction to the Lambeth Appeal among
the Free Churches, in a mystical vein which is typical of much
of Shakespeare's writing at this time.

> What the world needs is idealism... The saving salt of
> life is idealism and brotherhood. A Church which
> linked all men together in a common faith and devotion
> to Christ, which combined and transcended all races,
> nations and classes, could supply a very real bond of
> union, but not a Church which itself is split into
> fragments and itself violates the principle of fellow-
> ship... [86]

Shakespeare's shift of opinion concerning episcopacy is revealed very clearly in another passage:

> In gentle and tentative language the Lambeth Appeal
> claims that organic union can only be reached on the
> basis of episcopacy, and further, that it is 'the best
> instrument for maintaining the unity and continuity of
> of the Church'. At this stage it is quite easy for

> controversialists to make a number of debateable
> points. The historical fact, however, remains,
> that it became the instrument of the sub-apostolic
> church, and that out of an embryonic and rudimentary
> church order, taking various forms in different parts
> of the Roman Empire, Episcopacy emerged towards the
> end of the second century as the normal form...
>
> Only by bad history can we cite our Puritan fore-
> fathers against episcopacy for they believed in it
> and desired to remain under it within the Church of
> England...
>
> When all is said and done, the acceptance of epi-
> scopacy by the Free Churches in the light of their
> history would be a tremendous act. Yet we do not
> think it is too great a price to pay, interpreted
> as we have set it forth, for the incalculable
> blessing of fellowship.[87]

At this point Shakespeare's health began to give way, and
it seemed his contribution was over. But a brief recovery
made it possible for him to share in the arrangements for the
Baptist World Alliance Congress in Stockholm, 1923. He wrote
to Nathan Söderblom, Archbishop of Uppsala, with whom he was
in correspondence on other matters, asking him if he would in-
vite the BWA Congress to attend a service in the Cathedral.
Söderblom responded positively and insisted that Shakespeare
preach.   Shakespeare replied:

> Though we have not met, I have known for a long time
> that we were both interested in the same cause and
> were moved by the same principles of peace and unity.
> I accept your gracious invitation to preach... and
> realise the honour which your Grace has conferred
> upon me, though I accept it as a representative of
> the Congress... Your Grace will understand that I
> shall not preach as a Baptist but on those things
> which unite us in our common faith.[88]

When Shakespeare came to preach on that July Sunday in 1923
he chose as his text Luke 9.62: "No man having put his hand to
the plough and looking back is fit for the Kingdom of God".
It was a personal testimony, though most there did not realise
it, and it would be almost his last act as Secretary of the
Baptist Union.

> I have come to Stockholm to a Congress of Baptists,
> gathered from every nation under heaven - a Congress
> bearing a sectarian name, but I hope we shall meet in
> no sectarian spirit, and that our conference will be
> in harmony with that real Christian Unity and that
> spiritual fellowship in Christ, which is deeper than
> all our divisions and distinctions of name, creed,
> and nationality...

The opening half of the sermon is concerned with the necessity
of the ploughman to stay at his task despite what is happening
all around. It is a picture of the preacher, Shakespeare, with

his hand to the plough of Christian unity, refusing to look
back until the task is finished.

> It is hard work to be God's ploughman and to endure.
> It is hard work to maintain the first enthusiasm, the
> early devotion, sincerity of heart, purity of motive,
> unbroken courage and undimmed zeal...

> We have almost envied the ploughman on the fields,
> bathed in sunlight, breathing the fresh warm air.
> But watch him - he is in a lonely furrow, he must
> go straight and keep his eye fixed on the goal. He
> must plough deep and the share strikes stones which
> fling the handle against his side... The shadows
> lengthen and he is weary, but he must press on. The
> essential task of God's ploughman is to penetrate
> beneath the surface... All around as far as the eye
> can see, is the bare field. Not even the tiniest
> blade of wheat is above the surface. But the plough-
> man labours on... [89]

Shakespeare, whose eye had never been turned back, ploughed
on, committed, as from the beginning of his ministry, to the
task of the Church which is to "win the world to God",[90] and
noted "two great tasks to which the Church has set its hand
in these later days".

> The first is Peace, international peace. The Kingdom
> of God, says the great Apostle, is peace. Now the
> record of the Church in war and peace is a very bad
> one... Nearly all the Christian nations have been en-
> gaged for five years killing one another - a strange
> spectacle for heathen nations to watch. It is not
> for the Church to dogmatise upon the intricate prob-
> lems of international policy, but it must throw its
> weight in the scales for peace...

> The other problem of our time is Church Unity. Indeed
> the two are very closely related, for men will only
> deride churches which desire peace everywhere except
> among themselves... It is a hard field, full of stones
> and weeds and poisonous things. But I would bear my
> testimony to the change which has been wrought by the
> Appeal of the Bishops of the Church of England to all
> Christian people... At present we do not see which way
> God is leading us... we are seeking to realise the
> glorious vision of the Epistle to the Ephesians - to
> realise the great spiritual fact of our oneness in
> Christ. We have put our hand to the plough and in
> spite of the opposition of foes, and what is harder
> to bear, the misunderstanding of friends, we must not
> look back...

> We have been unprofitable servants, we have sometimes
> looked back, since in youth, we put our hand to the
> plough, but may God in His great mercy give us a place,
> even though a humble one in the Harvest Home.[91]

As Shakespeare walked to the pulpit to preach, the huge
Bible on the pulpit fell over the edge. It caused him great
consternation, and that, together with the constant interpol-
ations of the interpreter, made for an uninspired service.
Later that evening Shakespeare told J. C. Carlile, who had led
the service in the Cathedral, that the Bible's fall was a sign:
"My work is done". His nervous exhaustion and breakdown was
suddenly in evidence as he cried uncontrollably like a child.
He had a cerebral haemorrhage at the end of March 1925, and
eventually died, 12th March 1928.

Others must assess Shakespeare's life in its completeness,
but one thing is clear: any estimate of his work as Secretary
of the Baptist Union which ignores his ecumenical vision, his
deep sense of mission to a world broken by the 1914-18 War,
and his commitment to Lloyd George's Liberalism, will be a
caricature of a great Christian man, who, having put his hand
to the plough of Christian mission and unity, did not look
back, but planned and toiled for the Church of his own Baptist
faith, so that "when the grand festival of union comes she may
be led to the altar in radiant beauty, a bride anyone may be
proud to have".[92]

NOTES

1 J. H. Shakespeare, *The Churches at the Cross Roads. A Study in Church
   Unity*, London, Williams and Norgate, 1918. Hereafter referred to as
   CCR.

2 ibid. p.212.

3 J. C. Carlile, *My Life's Little Day*, London, Nisbet, 1935, p.177.

4 CCR p.7.

5 ibid. p.10 f.

6 ibid. p.16.

7 ibid. p.18.

8 ibid. p.22.

9 ibid. p.26.

10 ibid. p.28 f.

11 ibid. p.29.

12 ibid. p.31.

13 ibid. p.35 f.

14 ibid. p.36.

15 ibid. p.38.

16 ibid. p.40.

17 ibid. p.41.

18 ibid. p.55 f.

19 ibid. p.58.

20 ibid. p.61.

21 ibid. p.64.

22 ibid. p.67.

23 ibid. p.70.

24 ibid. p.71 f.

25 ibid. p.72.

26 ibid. p.76.

27 ibid. p.77.

28 ibid. p.79.

29 ibid. p.82.

30 ibid. p.94 f.

31 ibid. p.101 f.

32 ibid. p.104.

33 ibid. p.108.

34 ibid. p.111.

35 ibid. p.114.

36 ibid. p.116.

37 ibid. p.117.

38 ibid. p.123.

39 ibid. p.127.

40 ibid. p.139.

41 ibid. p.142.

42 ibid. p.149.

43 ibid. p.153.

44 ibid. p.166.

45 ibid. p.172.

46 ibid. p.173.

47 ibid. p.178.

48 ibid. p.182.

49 ibid. p.201.

50 ibid. p.204.

51 *St Mary's Magazine*, Norwich, Vol.III, No.34 (October 1898), p.85.

52 *Report of Church Congress*, Norwich, 1895, p.27.

53 ibid. p.445.

54 *Christian World*, 20th February 1896, p.136.

55 *St Mary's Church Book*, 1893, FC 6/4, Norfolk Record Office.

56 *An Election Sermon – The Duty of Christian Men in the Present Political Crisis*. Published, Norwich, p.3 f. Norfolk Record Office.

57 *CCR* p.151

58 *The Downfall of the Liberal Party, 1914-35,* Fontana, 1968, p.27.

59 Cf. the essay in this volume by D. W. Bebbington, "Baptists and Politics since 1914", p.

60 *Baptist Times*, 13th December 1918.

61 *Free Church Year Book*, 1916, p.9.

62 St Mary's Deacons' Minute Book 1836-1890, FC 6/7, Norfolk Record Office.

63 *Baptist and Congregational Pioneers*, London, Kingsgate Press, 1906.

64 ibid. p.15.

65 ibid. p.16.

66 ibid. p.125 f.

67 ibid. p.160.

68 ibid. p.10.

69 E. A. Payne, *Henry Wheeler Robinson,* London, Nisbet, 1946, p.51.

70 ibid. p.51.

71 Cf. E. K. H. Jordan, *Free Church Unity,* London, Lutterworth, 1956, p.127.

72 *Free Church Year Book*, 1911, p.165.

73 ibid. p.166.

74 ibid. p.168.

75 ibid. pp.19, 22 f.

76 *Free Church Year Book*, 1917, p.15.

77 *Baptist Times*, 3rd May 1918.

78 Tissington Tatlow MSS, Lambeth Palace Library.

79 *CCR*, p.178.

80 H. G. Wood, *Terrot Reaveley Glover*, Cambridge University Press, 1953, p.153.

81 Payne, op.cit.

82 *Baptist Times*, 9th May 1919.

83 J. W. Lockhart, *Cosmo Gordon Lang*, 1949, p.271.

84 ibid. p.274.

85 J. Marchant, ed., *The Coming Renaissance*, Cassell, 1922, p.87.

86 ibid. p.84.

87 ibid. pp.87-89.

88 N. Söderblom MSS, University of Uppsala Library, letters dated 11th October 1922, 9th February 1923.

89 MSS of sermon, p.5 f. [Copy in author's possession]

90 ibid. p.8.

91 ibid. p. 9 f.

92 *CCR* p.82.

ROGER HAYDEN

BAPTISTS IN FAITH AND ORDER

A STUDY IN BAPTISMAL CONVERGENCE

Anybody faced with the request to speak on such a wide and vague topic owes it both to himself and to his hearers to begin by defining much more precisely the content of what he intends to say. My intention is to indicate the extent of Baptist participation - particularly English Baptist partici- pation - in Faith and Order, and at the same time to try to show how over the years the subject of baptism has moved from the periphery towards the centre of Faith and Order discussion. Even this much more limited task is daunting, for it requires examination of the Faith and Order movement from its first World Conference at Lausanne in 1927 to the most recent Faith and Order Commission meeting at Lima in Peru in 1982. Whilst this paper is thus an introductory outline to a limited sub- ject, it is nevertheless a relevant topic for the churches are now faced with the request to respond to the 1982 Faith and Order Consensus Document entitled *Baptism, Eucharist and Ministry*.

This article, therefore, may be of some value in showing how the baptismal consensus has come about. Indeed a sub- title of this paper might well be "From Lausanne to Lima - from Comparison to Consensus: a study in Convergence". Lausanne began by setting side by side the various practices of the churches. Lima has tried to set down doctrinal con- sensus born out of fifty-five years of talking, working and praying together.

I

From Edinburgh 1910 to Edinburgh 1938: Preparing the Ground

Almost every ecumenical story of the past 60 years begins in the same way. "Once upon a time, in 1910, there was a Missionary Conference in Edinburgh...". This Edinburgh Con- ference was one which explicitly eschewed discussion on fun- damental doctrines of the faith, but grappled rather with most of the other questions of acting together in missionary enter- prise. After Edinburgh 1910, however, Charles Brent, an American Episcopalian of gentle disposition, immense courage, and considerable intellectual prowess, quickly recognised that relations amongst Christians would make little progress if the deep theological issues were not faced. He canvassed the idea of a World Conference on Faith and Order. Remarkable as it may now seem, at the Baptist Union Council in London in January 1914, three American Baptists, Dr Newman Smyth of New Haven, Dr Peter Ainslie of Baltimore, and Dr W. H. Roberts of Philadelphia, spoke of the plans for a World Conference on Faith and Order. The Baptist Union Council Minute reads "After protracted discussion, it was unanimously resolved to appoint a Baptist Commission of 14 persons to represent the Baptist Union of Great Britain and Ireland with a view to co-operating with the other Commissions with regard to the

arrangements'.[1] Both the Northern and the Southern Conven-
tions of Baptists in the United States of America also ans-
wered positively, but the First World War came all too soon,
and progress was halted. Hopes remained high that such a
Conference would be called as soon as conditions made it
possible, and Dr J. H. Shakespeare and Dr Pearce Gould were
appointed to the Executive Committee. In 1920 the Rev. Dr
J. E. Roberts, who had been Alexander McClaren's successor
in Manchester since 1903, and President of the Baptist Union
in 1918, represented the Baptist Union at a preliminary
Committee Meeting in Switzerland.

In 1919 J. H. Shakespeare's book *The Churches at the
Crossroads* had been published. This book with its very
positive and challenging statements concerning church relations had had a mixed reception. Many individuals welcomed
it, younger men rejoiced at its sentiments - the young Ernest
A. Payne, then aged 18, won a prize offered by the Baptist
Union in 1920 for an essay on the book! The book, however,
produced a counter-reaction to Shakespeare's ecumenical interests. One example of this counter reaction was the decision that, in spite of earlier interest, the Baptist Union
should not be represented at the Faith and Order Conference
planned for August 1927 at Lausanne. This decision set Baptists apart from the other British Churches in that the Church
of England, the Churches of Christ, Congregationalists, Methodists, and Presbyterians attended.

There were Baptists at Lausanne, however, representing the
Northern Convention of the United States of America, the
Seventh Day Baptist General Conference of the United States
of America, the Baptist Union of Ontario and Quebec, the
Seventh Day Baptist Churches of Holland, and the Baptist
Churches in Germany. The Southern Convention of the United
States reversed their original policy of co-operation during
the First World War. The reasons suggested by its historian,
W. W. Barnes, are two. First, because the inter-church world
movement of North America which was organised during the First
World War embarked upon grandiose and over ambitious tasks
including that of foreign mission, and, it is suggested,
"collapsed under its own weight'.[2] The second reason was that
the American War Department policy on religious work in the
Forces appeared to Southern Baptists to favour Roman Catholics
in an unconstitutional way. Over the years, the Southern
Baptists became more and more introverted. The Baptist Union
of Great Britain's decision not to participate disappointed
many, and J. E. Roberts and the historian W. T. Whitley
travelled to Lausanne at their own expense. The Baptist Union
also sent to Lausanne its 1926 reply to the Lambeth Appeal,
but it was not and could not be treated as a conference document, as it came from a non-participating group. Interestingly, however, J. E. Roberts conducted the worship of the conference on Thursday 4th August which was, in fact, the first
conference morning session.[3] At the conclusion of the conference, a Continuation Committee was set up and J. E. Roberts
accepted membership. It is important to note at this point,

that membership of Faith and Order has always been and remains still, on the basis of individual invitation, and not as a formal delegation or representative of a particular church. Naturally such invitations are with the agreement of the church to which a particular member belongs, but the invitation, nevertheless, remains personal.

The work of Lausanne was largely that of establishing doctrinal positions, noting emphases and differences, and, on the whole, stumbling across some agreements. Perhaps it will be helpful if at this point I remind you of the three periods which are usually distinguished in the history of Faith and Order.

1. 1927-1952 - Lausanne to Lund. The period of comparative ecclesiology, the main business of Faith and Order being the clarification of the doctrinal characteristics and beliefs of the various traditions.

2. 1952-1963 - Lund to Montreal. A period characterised by an attempt to seek an ecclesiological unity by reflection on the common basis of faith belonging to all traditions and by a return to the sources. During this period questions were raised particularly with regard to the relationship between Christ and the church and between Tradition and traditions, and the bearing of these issues upon the unity question.

3. 1963 onwards - Montreal to the present. A period which has emphasised the need for existential relationships in the locality, the common witness to the secularised world, and indeed a theological reflection on the world and humankind to which the unity of the church should be visibly related. Within this third period there are three further factors to be born in mind. The first is the developing Roman Catholic relationship to Faith and Order which grew after Vatican II. Secondly, the pressure from a variety of union schemes in different parts of the world. Third, the growing bi-lateral talks between World Confessional bodies, including, for example, the Baptist World Alliance, and the World Alliance of Reformed Churches.

How the question of Baptism reflects these three stages we shall see. But there are three particular dates and publications to note. The first is 1960, with the publication *One Lord, One Baptism*. Secondly, 1971 saw the publication of 'Baptism, Confirmation and Eucharist' in the Louvain document book, and finally 1982 saw the consensus document *Baptism, Eucharist and Ministry*.

At Lausanne, Dr Ashworth, pastor of the Baptist Church of the Redeemer, Yonkers, New York, spoke on the sacraments, emphasising the importance of the individual's response in faith and affirming the priesthood of all believers. Dr Ashworth said "in baptism the believer openly identifies himself with his Lord, dramatically setting forth in symbol that initial act of consecration by which he has died in penitence with Christ to the old life of sin, and by the

power of God has been raised from death to walk in the new
life with the Christ who is the source of it".[4]   The Lausanne
statement on baptism occupies five lines and is cautious in
the extreme.[5]

When Dr Roberts died in 1929, M. E. Aubrey took his place
on the Continuation Committee and was subsequently to play a
highly significant part, not only in Faith and Order but also
in the developing of the World Council of Churches over the
next 20 years.

Between Lausanne 1927 and the Faith and Order Conference
at Edinburgh in 1937, the Continuation Committee met regularly.   The Lausanne Report was sent out in 1928 and on the
death of Charles Brent in 1929, William Temple, Archbishop of
York, was elected Chairman.   The churches began to reply to
and to comment upon the Lausanne documents.   Thus church
participation in Faith and Order is no new thing as some recent members of Faith and Order seem to think.   Gradually
with the help of the replies from the churches, and of returned questionnaires from the churches, the themes for the
next Faith and Order Conference began to emerge.   Most particularly they had to do with the doctrine of grace, the sacraments, the nature and the purpose of the church.   These were
crystallised out for Edinburgh under four headings:

    The Grace of our Lord Jesus Christ
    The Church of Christ and the Word of God
    The Church of Christ and the Ministry and Sacraments
    The Church's Unity in Life and Worship.

At Edinburgh in 1937 there were seventeen Baptists present,
five from the Northern Baptist Convention, four from the
Southern Baptists, five from the Baptist Union of Great Britain and Ireland, two from Scotland and one from Canada.   The
five from the Baptist Union of Great Britain and Ireland were
Dr Gilbert Laws, Mr C. T. LeQuesne, Dr J. H. Rushbrooke, Dr
Hugh Martin, and Dr M. E. Aubrey.   The last-named had a sig-
nificant part in the Conference in that he was Chairman of
Section IV, the section on "The Church's Unity in Life and
Worship".   After Edinburgh Aubrey was not only a member of
the Continuation Committee but also of the Executive Committee
of that body and more significantly he was the alternate to
J. H. Oldham on the Constituent Committee set up jointly by
the Life and Work Conference in Oxford (1937) and Faith and
Order to prepare the way for a proposed World Council of
Churches.   Interestingly Dr Ashworth, a Baptist, was Chairman
of the Committee to draft the Edinburgh affirmation of Union -
which was really the word to the churches.[6]   It was a distinguished Committee, including Bishop Azariah of Dornakal,
Professor C. H. Dodd, and others, and is described by Rouse
and Neill as "a memorable affirmation".[7]

So far as baptism is concerned, the Edinburgh Report is
neither very hopeful nor very helpful, but reflects probably
the true position.   There are only two brief paragraphs on it
and even the first statement concerning the meaning of baptism
has a footnote with a Baptist comment and addition.[8]

At Edinburgh there were one or two considerable interven-
tions and addresses by Baptists. Dr Harold Phillips of the
Northern Baptist Convention spoke forcibly on the subject of
the equality before God of the individual. "In a word, we do
not believe in the priesthood of a class merely, but in the
priesthood of all believers, every individual competent under
God". He went on to argue strongly for the freedom which
rests with every Christian man. With a wry comment he said
"The Baptist creed is something like the British Constitution;
it is unwritten, and hence does not cause so much trouble as
the American Constitution seems to be causing at the present
time".[9]

In the receiving of the Section Reports, Mr C. T. LeQuesne
spoke on the Report relating to the Ministry and Sacraments,
remarking:

> To the Baptist delegates in this Section, it seemed
> that the Report dealing with the Ministry would
> suggest to most readers that all the bodies here
> represented were content to accept the proposition
> that Episcopacy is essential to the United Church.
> We felt that it was only honest to say that many
> among the Baptists, and probably among the other
> Free Church bodies cannot be said to be prepared
> to accept that proposition...[10]

Dr Rushbrooke and C. T. LeQuesne together successfully moved
an addition to the Report on the matter of Apostolic Succession, which read "other communions, while unaccustomed to use
the term Apostolic Succession, would accept it as meaning
essentially or even exclusively, the maintenance of the
apostles' witness through the true preaching of the Gospel,
the right administration of the Sacraments, and the perpetuation of the Christian life in the Christian community".[11]

It is worth reflecting that these two comments are still
germane to the ecumenical discussion.

II

From Edinburgh to Montreal: Laying the Foundations

In 1938 the Continuation Committee set up two Commissions to
study the Doctrine of the Church - one European and the other
American. In 1939 a Commission on Ways of Worship and another
one on Intercommunion were initiated. But then came the
Second World War. During the war William Temple died, as did
A. E. Garvie, the distinguished Congregationalist, Principal
of Hackney and New College, who had been Vice Chairman of
Faith and Order since Lausanne. In 1947 the Continuation
Committee elected Archbishop Brillioth of Uppsala to the
Chair and after Amsterdam in 1948 the Continuation Committee
became the first Commission of Faith and Order within the
World Council of Churches.

Theology had moved on since 1937, particularly under the
influence of Barth and Brunner. Their writings had had an

effect upon the question of baptism. Both of them, particularly Barth, began to challenge the practice of Infant Baptism
on biblical and theological grounds. The Church of England
was also disturbed concerning the relationship of baptism to
confirmation (and/or vice versa) and indeed began to wonder
about the concept of Christian initiation. Preparations were
already in hand, however, for a third World Conference on
Faith and Order at Lund in Sweden. At Clarens in Switzerland,
a new Commission met and there were present from England in
1951, C. T. LeQuesne, Ernest A. Payne (who had now replaced
Aubrey on the Faith and Order Commission) and myself, as a
youth delegate! The Theological Commission on the Church
initiated by the Continuation Committee in 1938 had produced
a Report, and amongst those who had helped on that Commission
as Baptists was C. T. LeQuesne with P. W. Evans as a consul-
tant. So far as baptism was concerned, little of moment was
said. There is simply a statement about the dominical nature
of the sacrament and a further statement about the differences
of understanding of that sacrament. Lund, however, was to
change all that.

The third World Conference on Faith and Order was held at
Lund from 15th to 28th August 1952. Fourteen Baptists were
present including five from Great Britain, namely Ernest A.
Payne, C. T. LeQuesne, Kenneth Dykes, Ingli James (representing the Baptist Union of New Zealand) and myself as a Youth
Delegate - though 'youth' was rather more generously interpreted then than it would be now! Godfray LeQuesne was also
present as a visitor and shared in some of the work of the
youth delegation. Two theologians stand out in the memory.
One was Edmund Schlink from Germany and the other was Thomas
Torrance from Scotland - a former pupil of Barth. Naturally
one cannot give a full report of the Lund Conference, but
one or two quotations are important to illustrate the way in
which it affected ecumenical thinking, particularly on the
subjects with which we are concerned.

The first quotation should, however, be a reminder of the
important Lund dictum to which more and more reference is now
being made in the light of the failure of the recent Covenanting talks in England. All too often, this dictum is quoted
out of context. The Lund Conference included it in a section
which stands at the beginning of its Report, entitled "A Word
to the Churches". Here is the dictum in context.

> We would, therefore, earnestly request our churches
> to consider whether they are doing all they ought
> to do to manifest the oneness of the People of God.
> Should not our churches ask themselves whether they
> are showing sufficient eagerness to enter into con-
> versation with other Churches, and whether they
> should not act together in all matters, except those
> in which deep differences of conviction compel them
> to act separately? Should they not acknowledge the
> fact that they often allow themselves to be separated
> from each other by secular forces and influences
> instead of witnessing together to the sole Lordship

of Christ, who gathers His People out of all nations, races and tongues?[12]

Within the Report baptism is spoken of as one of the "marks of the Church's unity".[13] In the course of Schlink's address he said: "As baptised persons we have 'died unto sin', even if we daily admit that we are sinners and have every reason to ask our Father who is in heaven to forgive us our trespasses. As our belief that in Baptism we have died with Christ unto sin transcends the obstacle of our visible sins, as in our belief in the crucified we are certain that as sinners we are justified before God, so we are also certain that in spite of all our divisions, we are one in Christ".[14]

Within the volume prepared for the InterCommunion discussion at Lund there was an important emphasis by Torrance upon the relationship between baptism and eucharist:

> If Baptism means actual incorporation into the Body
> of Christ, and already means through the Word a con-
> tinuous feeding upon the flesh and blood of Christ,
> as our Lord so clearly stated in the Fourth Gospel,
> who are we to deny those so baptised, renewal of
> their incorporation in the Body of Christ, provided
> that they are sincere?... To refuse the Eucharist
> to those baptised into Christ Jesus and incorporated
> into His Resurrection Body, amounts either to a
> denial of the transcendant reality of Holy Baptism
> or to attempted schism within the Body of Christ.[15]

This particular quotation reflects not only the relating between baptism and eucharist but also a recognition of the ecclesiological context concerning baptism and indeed the relation of ecclesiology to the incarnation in the body of Christ.

The Faith and Order Commission which was set up at Lund contained seven Baptists, including Ernest Payne and C. T. LeQuesne, with the former being a member of the Working Committee. At the Working Committee held at Bossey in 1953, Torrance renewed his plea for a thinking about the relationship between Christ and sacraments, christology and unity.

> The church needed to be considered in relationship
> to the doctrine of Christ and the Holy Spirit. We
> cannot think through the Doctrine of Christ and His
> Body without going more deeply into the Doctrine of
> the Sacraments. We are given the Sacraments to help
> us state and show things that cannot otherwise be
> stated, and yet we are trying to describe the relation
> between Christ and His Body without using the very
> means that are put into our hands to do so.[16]

At Lund there had been a suggestion, later put into practice, for a Commission to be set up to discuss christology and ecclesiology. The outcome was that a Theological Commission was set up on *Christ and the Church* which, as it developed over the years, found itself more and more involved with the question of baptism. A preparatory study was carried out on

the subject by the European Section of that Theological Commission and this study was presented to the Working Committee
of the Commission of Faith and Order at New Haven, Connecticut
in 1957.   It dealt considerably with baptism.   It begins thus:

> Within the disunity of the Churches, the unity of
> baptism has remained.   With few exceptions, the
> Churches mutually recognised the baptisms which
> they administer, and do not repeat the Sacrament
> when there is transmission from one Church to
> another.   We of the member Churches of the World
> Council have to emphasise afresh what this unity
> maintained in disunity means for our inter-relation-
> ships.   The fathers of the first Ecumenical Synod at
> Nicaea, confessing one Christ, found themselves com-
> pelled to reaffirm the one baptism in accordance
> with the teaching of the New Testament.   We also,
> making the same confession, and in obedience to the
> same teaching, confess "the one baptism for the
> remission of sins".   In all our churches baptism is
> administered in accordance with the command given
> in Matthew 28:19-20 "Go ye there, and make disciples
> of all nations, baptising them into the name of the
> Father and of the Son and of the Holy Ghost: teach-
> ing them to observe all things whatsoever I com-
> manded you: and lo, I am with you alway, even unto
> the end of the world.[17]

Further on in the Working Paper there is a statement
about baptism as follows:

> There belong inseparably together the one body, one
> spirit, one hope, one Lord, one faith, one baptism,
> one God and Father (Eph.4:4).   In virtue of this
> interconnection the confession of one baptism has
> unavoidable implications for the interrelationships
> of divided churches.   In baptism we are all incor-
> porated into the fullness of Christ.
>
> (a)   The unity of baptism commits us to common con-
> fession of the great acts of God which he has accom-
> plished once and for all in Christ, and which by the
> word and sacraments he performs upon the world and
> will continue to do so.
>
> (b)   The unity of baptism commits us to common
> obedience in discipleship to Christ: both in service
> to one another and in service to the world.
>
> (c)   The unity of baptism commits us to acknowledge
> that the continuity as well as the unity of the
> church has its foundation in baptismal incorporation
> to Christ.
>
> (d)   The unity of baptism commits us to remove the
> obstacles to manifesting the one body of Christ in
> the world by common reception of the body and blood
> of Christ in the eucharist.

(e)   The unity of baptism commits us to remove the obstacles to reciprocal recognition of the ministries by which Christ wills to hold together his body.

(f)   The unity of baptism commits us to acknowledge that the ministry of Word and Sacrament has its place only within the corporate ministry of the whole body.[18]

There was considerable discussion on the Paper as a result of which there was produced a much more cautious statement and it was agreed that the following issues should be given particular attention within the Commission on *Christ and the Church*.

(a)   The corporate baptism of the church in the death and resurrection of Jesus Christ and the rite of water baptism in the historical life of the church.

(b)   The difference of theology between those who practise infant baptism and those who restrict their practice to believer's baptism.

(c)   The nature of sacramental efficacy.

(d)   The place of baptism in the process of Christian initiation as a whole.

(e)   The relevance of pastoral responsibility to the whole question of diverse forms and doctrines of baptism.

The conclusion following these five questions is as follows: "When these questions have been considered, we may more profitably deal with the implications of baptism for Christian unity".[19]

Between 1957 and 1959 the Theological Commissions on *Christ and the Church*, both in Europe and America, worked on according to their terms of reference and each Commission recognised more and more that it was necessary to say something both about the meaning of baptism and also its relationship to the unity of the church, most particularly to that unity seen in the christological context.   A report entitled *The Meaning of Baptism* was prepared by a joint meeting of the two Theological Commissions and was before the members of the Working Committee on Faith and Order in 1959 at Spittal in Austria.   This report had an introductory paper to it which had been distributed and written by Anders Nygren.

At Spittal the subject was introduced by Ernest Payne in the context of the discussion on the implications of baptism for Christian Unity.   This introduction by Ernest Payne was highly significant and important.   It is printed in full in the minutes of the Working Committee in Spittal.[20]   After drawing attention to the comments made by Torrance and others at Lund, Ernest Payne goes on to show how there had been a growing interest in the question of baptism and unity reflected in the Faith and Order Commission at New Haven in 1957 of which we have already spoken.   He drew attention also to a number of further publications including the Church of Scotland report on baptism which was prepared in 1955 with further comments and versions in 1956, 1957 and 1958.   He also referred to the work which had gone on in Europe in the Reformed and Lutheran

traditions discussing baptism. This particular discussion
had set down a series of theses under the headings "Who acts
in baptism?", "What happens to us in baptism?", "How does
this happen in baptism?", "How do we use the baptismal rite?".
He goes on to comment that these discussions indicate that
members of this Reformed Lutheran consultation recognise that
the problem of infant baptism needs further discussion.

Particularly interesting is that he draws attention to work
amongst Baptists on the subject, most notably Neville Clark's
monograph entitled *An Approach to the Theology of the Sacraments* and also to the same writer's essay in the book edited
by Alec Gilmore entitled *Christian Baptism*. Payne points out
that Neville Clark, like other writers of the time, is emphasising the importance that the theology of baptism "must be
written round the two poles of the baptism of Jesus at Jordan
and its fulfilment in his death, resurrection and ascension".
Payne goes on to indicate how the Anglicans also had been
looking at the whole question of baptism and confirmation and
that they had come to the conclusion that in the New Testament
adult baptism is the norm and it is only in the light of this
fact that the doctrine and practice of baptism can be understood.

Payne points out Bishop Nygren's comment that the idea of
recognising the baptism of other churches so widely canvassed
was not so much due to a common view of baptism but was all
too often connected with the fact that so little significance
was attached to baptism that there was no need for it to become a point of controversy between the churches! Nygren
believed that Faith and Order was now presented with a challenge to a deeper study of the meaning of baptism in the wide
context of the salvation history which proceeds from Christ
and is present and active in his church.

Payne then goes on to indicate that this sort of statement
links with the re-drawing of terms of reference which had been
discussed and presented at New Haven and he concludes with
this comment: "At the present time no church is particularly
easy in conscience, I think, regarding baptism. All we can
do is, in the name of the one true church, to continue the
ecumenical discussion". [21]

In the discussion which followed, Professor Schlinck commented that if the Faith and Order Commission could ever reach
a consensus on baptism, particularly on the basis of the document presented, that is, *The Meaning of Baptism*, this would be
a major accomplishment in itself! [22]

The document *The Meaning of Baptism* came to the full Faith
and Order Commission at St Andrews in 1960. The Commission,
by this time, had been strengthened Baptist-wise by the
appointment of Dr Champion. The St Andrews Commission had
before it in its discussion on *The Meaning of Baptism*, two
introductory papers. The first was given by Dr Jakob of Berlin
who was from East Germany, on "Problems of Baptismal Practice
in Areas under Communist Rule Today". [23] The importance of this
particular address is that it faced the Commission fairly and

squarely with the contextual nature of the baptismal issue.
He points out that there has been developed a secular naming
ceremony for children in the East German context and this was
forcing the re-thinking of baptismal practice, and there had
been a study of baptism in the context of East Germany from
which emerged certain points:

> The findings of theology and the present practice of
> the church compel us to revise the church's baptismal
> practice:
>
> (a)   Baptism of adults should be permitted as a valid
> order even for members of Christian families.
>
> (b)   The church must no longer insist on infant
> baptism and the orders must be altered accordingly.
> The following ordinances in the present orders are
> particularly objected to.
>
> 1.   The congregation shall urge that children of
> Christian parents be baptised during the first weeks
> after they are born.
>
> 2.   Children who die before they are baptised can
> have a church funeral provided that their premature
> or sudden death is the sole cause why they have not
> been baptised.
>
> (c)   It is in accordance with the freedom of the
> Gospel to practice different forms of baptism.
>
> (d)   In all cases in which infant baptism is practised
> in future, the nature of Christian baptism must be
> clearly explained to the parents beforehand, the
> possibility of adult baptism must be pointed out, and
> if necessary they may be encouraged to postpone the
> baptism; the baptism must take place in the presence
> of the congregation; and the church must be in a
> position to carry out its responsibility for instruc-
> ting the children who have been baptised in the
> evangelical faith.
>
> (e)   All members of the Protestant Church must be
> given the opportunity to ask the congregation to
> pray for their newborn children and to care for them
> even if they have not received infant baptism.[24]

This interesting paper was then followed by one by Neville
Clark who introduced the document *The Meaning of Baptism*
which had had a preliminary discussion the previous year at
Spittal in Austria.   It is perhaps worthwhile noting that as
in 1959 when the subject was introduced by Ernest Payne so
now in 1960 the subject at St Andrews was introduced by a
Baptist, Neville Clark.   Before we consider his introduction,
word must be said about the document itself.   The actual full
document is entitled *One Lord, One Baptism*, and contains two
papers, one entitled "The Divine Trinity, and the Unity of
the Church", the second entitled "The Meaning of Baptism".
It is interesting that these two papers should be together
and should be seen in relationship to each other.   Those who

shared in the production of the whole document included
George Beasley Murray, who acted as Secretary of the European
Group, and included such significant theologians as Anders
Nygren, Geoffrey Lampe, Oscar Cullmann, Edmund Schlink, T. F.
Torrance and John Marsh. There is a particularly important
development in the consideration of baptism in the section
entitled "Baptism and Salvation History". Five crucial points
are indicated within the History. These are:

> The Baptism of John,
> The Baptism of Jesus,
> His Death and Resurrection,
> The significance of Pentecost for the church,
> The Baptism of the individual.

The final chapter which raises theological implications
and questions notes four particular areas for consideration:
the meaning of participation, the relation of faith to baptism,
the significance of baptism for the whole of life, the eschatological aspect of its relation to the Lord's Supper and Confirmation, and baptism as call to service. Under the final
section "Baptism as Call to Service", three sub-headings are
noted: "To be baptised is to live in and for Christ"; "To be
baptised is to live in and for the church"; "To be baptised
is to live in and for the world".

The conclusion of the report emphasises that to begin considering baptism in its relationship to salvation history
means that the other rites of the church, including the
eucharist, can be seen "as dependent upon and in various ways
renewing, or more specifically expressing the fullness of
baptism itself. Such a view is not intelligible if we think
of baptism as a self-sufficient rite; it is demanded inescap-
ably if we think of baptism as the expression of the whole
salvation history ... To begin with baptism considered in
this way will thus lead to a clearer and more genuinely
theological understanding of sacraments".[25] The conclusion
goes on to say that "This consideration is highly significant
both for the practical life of the church and for the unity
of the church and in both respects the church has suffered
severely from the fact that the christological significance
of baptism has received so little attention".[26] The conclusion goes on to illustrate two applications. One is that a
serious penetration into the meaning of baptism would give
preaching and teaching both a centrally focussed content and
a new breadth together with an insight which clarifies and
unifies the whole of Christian life. It is also of decided
importance to pastoral care to be able to say to a troubled
human being "You are baptised". It is secondly important in
the application to be able to point to the deepest meaning of
baptism as participation in Christ and through baptism we are
members of the Body of Christ, planted in Christ already, who
is our unity.

It was this document which Neville Clark introduced at St
Andrews.[27] He welcomed it warmly particularly for its title
and for the importance of relating baptism to salvation history. But went on to raise certain points that he believed

were unclear in the document. One was the relationship
between the theological explication of baptism and the
exegesis of the biblical text. He comments that it is important to recognise that "discrepancies between the biblical
exegete and the theologian (also biblical) are sufficiently
great still to be disquieting". He argues further that it is
necessary to take care lest we lose history in theology and
relate baptism so closely to the cross and resurrection that
the baptism of Jordan misses its measure of independence. He
argued that there were three fundamental sub-sections relating
to the subject. First, the baptism of Jesus; second,
the cross, resurrection and ascension events taken altogether;
third, Pentecost and Christian baptism. He went on further
to argue that the issue between infant and believer's baptism
is not an issue which is simply a controversy about baptism
but is a controversy about the Gospel itself, and argues that
therefore this particular controversy is still nowhere near a
solution in that document with which the Commission was faced,
in spite of the helpful nature of the document itself.

In a similar way the question of confirmation as a separate
rite is absent from the consideration in the document. He
argued that the report on the whole lacks a sustained theological argument and a theological examination of kingdom,
church and the nature of redemption.

The discussion which followed produced a number of interesting points, not least that in Romans 6, which is one of
the great biblical texts used in the report, there is an important question and a proper tension between the eschatological context of that particular text and the present
ethical demand.

A sub-committee was set up at St Andrews to look at the
meaning of baptism and the various comments which came first
from the discussion and then from the sub-committee itself
pointed to the necessity for further work.   The sub-committee
made general comments which pinpointed certain really important issues. Space permits a mention of only some of them.

   1.   We believe that the controversy between the
   advocates of adult and infant baptism is not a mere
   confessional controversy but must be seen in a context
   which makes apparent its true theological implications.

   2.   We believe that the increasing degree to which
   baptism has become associated with cultural phenomena,
   both in the east and in the west, makes it necessary
   to study baptismal discipline with particular care.
   It is apparent that the duty of accepting and dis-
   charging pastoral responsibility in this area must
   seriously be laid upon the churches.

   3.   Certain members of the sub-committee feel that
   the report does not sufficiently emphasise the priority
   of divine grace in dealing with infant baptism and that
   the idea of the covenant which embraces the family
   should be carefully included.

4. The eschatological dimension, mentioned in the report, might be more fully developed and more clearly expressed. Moreover, the ethical implications of baptism are not sufficiently emphasised. We believed that these two need to be kept in the closest possible relation, one to the other, since the eschatological dimension embraces the ethical. [28]

We have dealt in some detail with this particular document because the most recent document published more than twenty years after quite clearly picks up and re-emphasises these very same points. It is important to understand that the present document is one that has developed out of the previous discussion on baptism within the Faith and Order movement.

III

Montreal to Lima: Beginning to build

In 1963 there was a fourth World Conference on Faith and Order in Montreal. The Faith and Order Commission was further strengthened by the addition of Dr Russell Aldwinkle and there were present at Montreal some eighteen Baptists including from England George Beasley Murray, Victor Hayward, Ernest Payne, Leonard Champion and Gwenyth Hubble. Montreal was held some eighteen months after the New Delhi Assembly in the World Council of Churches at which there had been a further sign of Roman Catholic interest in the whole ecumenical discussion. The Montreal conference has been variously commented upon. Most people are agreed that it represented both a point of arrival and also one of departure. It marked a point where there was a movement from the second phase in Faith and Order which emphasised the consideration of Christ and the church, the christological and ecclesiological, to the necessity for common witness, for theological reflection on the world and of the church and its practices set in the context of the world. Already we have seen signs of this development taking place in the discussion of the documents we have already dealt with. There were also those who felt that Montreal was some- what confused in its thinking. Certainly it is generally agreed that the broader spectrum of churches participating, notably the Romans, and the continuing and developing Orthodox presence did complicate matters somewhat. It is perhaps significant that there has never been another Faith and Order World Conference though there is now some suggestion that there should be a further World Conference in the late 1980s, probably some twenty-five years after Montreal.

Baptism itself did not get too much of a hearing in Mon- treal. The introduction to the report of the Theological Commission on Christ and the Church which had, as we have seen, produced the document *One Lord, One Baptism*, comments:

An endeavour was made to view baptism in the light of the Christological significance which it seemed to possess in the New Testament. The result was instruc- tive in cutting behind the traditional confessional

issues to the Christological emphases associated with
baptism in the New Testament and we found an unexpected
measure of agreement among the members of the Commission.
If we did not solve all the difficulties (some of the
acutest in the life of the churches were hardly considered), the mode of approach to baptism which emerged
merits further exploration by the churches.[29]

It is probably true to say that Montreal revealed that the
agreements had been reached over the ten years since Lund by
people who growingly knew and respected each other and understood each other. In the stark light of theological discussion in Montreal it became evident that the agreements were
not quite as real as had at first appeared. The present
writer served, between Lund and Montreal, on the European
section of the Worship Commission and undoubtedly the conclusions reached there were reached over the years in theological
discussion by people who were growingly friends. This may
well reflect and say something about the problems of Faith
and Order Methodology. Certainly it was this sort of issue
which helped to trigger the next period of Faith and Order
work which made it clear that that which was talked about in
the theological discussion must be much more clearly related
to the realities of life of the church in a growingly secular
world.

Immediately after Montreal there was a period when the
discussion on baptism faded somewhat into the background. I
joined the Faith and Order Commission formally as a member at
Aarhaus in Denmark in 1964, when Ernest Payne found that the
pressure of his other ecumenical responsibilities meant that
he must resign from the Commission. With his resignation Dr
Champion became a member of the Working Committee. At Aarhaus
there were still seven Baptists on the Commission, including
Dale Moody, a Southern Convention Baptist from the United
States. Discussions in Faith and Order at Aarhaus tended to
move in somewhat different directions than previously although
it may be argued that in some sense there was a working out
of the implications that had become evident from what had gone
on before and during the Montreal discussions. The main discussions centred upon the themes of Creation, New Creation and
the Unity of the Church; upon Christ the Holy Spirit and the
Ministry; upon Spirit, Order and Organisation. It is perhaps
worthy of significance that the work in the study commission
between Aarhaus in 1964 and the Commission meeting at Bristol
in 1967 on these three subjects, or various aspects of them,
contained all too few Baptist participants, and even the
group that continued to discuss the eucharist did not see it
very clearly in connection with baptism.

At the Bristol Commission meeting in 1967 it was quite
clear that it was going to be necessary for the eucharist discussion to include relationship between that sacrament and
baptism. The Bristol meeting received a warning from the
Director of Faith and Order, Lukas Vischer, that baptism must
be borne in mind for it was growingly becoming an issue in
union discussions and it was also seen as an important part

in the discussion which was developing on the subject of
conciliarity, which was a study of the nature of relationships
in councils based upon an understanding of the history of the
church in which baptism is seen to be "the sacramental bond
which still joined in the past the divided groups".[30]

These words were undoubtedly heeded because when the Faith
and Order Commission met at Louvain in Belgium in 1971 there
was a significant development on the whole issue of baptism.
A group had been discussing baptism, confirmation and the
eucharist. On this group there was one Baptist, namely
Gunther Wagner, from the Ruschlikon Seminary in Switzerland.
The document produced by the group, however, is extremely important in the development of the whole discussion of baptism
and there was an extremely important discussion which took
place at Louvain.   The report *Baptism, Confirmation and
Eucharist* which came to Louvain, begins with this comment:

> The Report, *One Lord, One Baptism,* had been concerned
> primarily with establishing a common understanding of
> baptism without as yet drawing concrete conclusions
> for the Church's liturgy and practice.   The new study
> on baptism, confirmation and eucharist needs to include
> these aspects and to explore whether agreement could
> be reached upon them.[31]

The document presented to Louvain first of all reviews the
present practices of the churches using the old comparative
method but it then goes on to talk about the question of how
to approach the issues bearing in mind the problem of biblical
authority, the church authority which comes from the Early
Church and the tradition which has developed since.   It goes
on to pick up the important connection between christology,
ecclesiology and the understanding and practice of baptism,
and develops the implication of baptismal life, that is the
life in the spirit, for what we would call responsible church
membership.   There is a consideration of the liturgy, that is
the actual practice - the how - of the baptismal rite, and the
importance of various elements being present within the rite.
It raises the question also of the unity of baptismal initiation; not only unity of the whole process but also the relationship between the elements in the process and begins to
discuss under this heading the issue of mutual recognition of
believer's baptism and infant baptism and the relationship
between baptism, confirmation and admission to the eucharist.
The report also made it very clear that it might be argued
that there are already some ecumenical agreements on baptism.
Indeed, it even lists certain points of agreement:

1.   That baptism is a sacrament instituted by Christ.

2.   That baptism is a participation in the death and
resurrection of Christ.

3.   That baptism is a gift of the spirit and incorporation into the church.

4.   That in baptism there is a relationship between
faith and baptism itself.

5. That there is general agreement on the administration of baptism and most particularly the elements
within any order of baptism which must involve acknow-
ledgement of God's initiative, declaration of the forgiveness of sins, prayer for the Holy Spirit, renunciation of evil, profession of faith in Christ, affirmation that the person baptised is incorporated into the
Body of Christ and baptism in water in the Name of
the Trinity.

6. That there is a universality of baptism and that it
is unique and once for all.

7. That in baptism there is a commitment and witness
to Christ.

8. That there is a close link between baptism and the
eucharist.[32]

There was a considerable discussion of this document at
Louvain. There are two particular points which were discussed
and which became even more important and more relevant in the
decade since Louvain. One is the effect of the age in which
we live with its secularism and atheism upon the question as
to who may be baptised. This is the issue that Dr Jakob
vividly raised soon after the Lund conference. The other is
the question of those who wished to renew their baptismal
vows by a personal profession of faith.

Most important of all, however, was the decision of Louvain
that there really needed to be a consideration as to whether
there could not be some consensus document prepared on baptism,
eucharist and ministry. In the end it was decided that it
would be a proper work of Faith and Order to attempt to
develop the consensus which had already been suggested at
Louvain on baptism and to see if it were possible to include
also eucharist and ministry.

At Louvain the present writer found himself elected to the
then Working Committee of Faith and Order. After Louvain
there remained eight Baptist members on the Faith and Order
Commission but only the present writer from this country.
Between Louvain and the Working Committee at Utrecht in 1972
a further tidying up was done on documents concerning the
attempt at consensus on baptism and work begun on eucharist.
It was decided also that the documents thus far should be
sent to all member churches in the World Council to see if
comments could be elicited from them.

The next Commission meeting met in Ghana in 1974. At this
meeting a first consensus document on baptism, eucharist and
ministry was drafted. The text was produced after considerable work and discussion and in particular the section on
baptism caused some difficulty to Baptist members present.
There was general agreement on the definition of baptism
itself and on the implications of the sacrament, but there
was some feeling that the document spoke too glibly of a
common baptism which unites us all in Christ. There were
those who felt that the points of difference between infant

and believer's baptism as stated did not go to the heart of
the theological divide. At one point in the discussion it
was suggested that there should be a Baptist footnote to the
consensus text. Not surprisingly some pressure was brought
to bear on the Baptists about this and in the end it was
agreed that, provided it was made clear in the Introduction
that the document was not a consensus of all that was in the
text but rather a summary of shared convictions and perspec-
tives to lead the churches closer together, then the document
might be accepted as it said. The document when it came out
was entitled *One Baptism, One Eucharist and a Mutually Recognised Ministry*.[33] In 1975 it was brought to the Fifth
Assembly of the World Council of Churches in Nairobi and was
commended to be sent formally to all the member churches
asking for specific response from each member church.

At Nairobi the Faith and Order Commission was reconstituted.
The new structure of the World Council of Churches had trans-
formed the working committee of Faith and Order into the
Standing Commission and the Commission itself into the Plenary
Commission. The number of Baptists on the Commission was
reduced to five. This was due largely to the cut in size of
the Commission itself and the present writer became the only
Baptist on the Standing Commission.

The document, known as B.E.M., which was sent to the
churches contained a definition of the meaning of baptism
under three headings, first - Participation in the death and
resurrection of Christ; second - the gift of the Spirit and
incorporation into the Body of Christ; third - Baptism and
Faith. The implications of baptism were stated to be three-
fold, a bond of unity, an imperative to lead to eucharistic
sharing and a commitment and witness to Christ. Amongst the
recommendations of the document was one that Baptists should
give further consideration to the place of the child in God's
providence for His church, whilst those practising infant
baptism should guard against indiscriminate infant baptism.[34]

The Baptist Union of Great Britain and Ireland made a
response to this document and suggested that there was need
for genuine, rather than apparent, agreement and indicated
that the cracks had been plastered over at certain points,
for example, in the relationship between scriptural authority
and ecclesial authority. Secondly, there was failure to recognise that at the heart of the infant and believer's baptism
issue lay ecclesiological differences. Thirdly, there was in
the document an over-simplification of the question of so-
called re-baptism.

All the replies to the document from the member churches
were received and considered at a special consultation in
Switzerland in 1977. It was clear that there was general
agreement on the statement on the meaning of baptism but that
much more work needed to be done on the following points:

    1.   The authority for the practice of baptism.

    2.   The co-existence of both practices, infant and
believer's baptism, in one church.

3. So far as the two practices are concerned a number
of issues needed consideration, (a) the meaning of
faith as applied to both practices (b) the ecclesiological implications lying behind both practices
(c) the developing practice of the blessing of infants.

4. The question of confirmation required much more
consideration.

5. The meaning of baptism in the Holy Spirit.

6. The issue of contextuality.[35]

Amongst the recommendations was that a consultation with
Baptists to explore the issues involved in the debate on infant baptism and believer's baptism should, if possible, be
set up by the Faith and Order Commission. The Standing Commission of Faith and Order meeting at Loccum revised further
the texts of *Baptism, Eucharist and Ministry* at the Plenary
Commission in Bangalore in 1978, and at both these meetings
Baptists were deeply involved particularly in the baptism
work.

At the end of March 1979 a consultation was held at Louisville, hosted by the Southern Convention, between groups
representing the Baptists and those practising infant baptism.
The report of the Louisville Consultation is available for all
to read and study. In the *Baptist Quarterly* of 1980 volume 28
No. 5, the present writer has an article describing the event.[36]
There is thus neither space nor necessity to repeat in any
detail what was written there save to emphasise that in hind-
sight the Louisville Consultation did get the questions right
and also was right in its emphasis upon contextuality. It
may also be commented that the holding of the Consultation at
all marked a highly important stage in the ecumenical discussion. As I wrote then, "the setting up of the Louisville
Consultation recognised that the question of baptismal practice is not to be decided, of course, by weight of numbers
for each practice, but by the recognition of the equal importance of considering each practice".[37]

After the Louisville Consultation and after further Standing
Commission meetings in 1979 and 1981, together with the final
meeting of the Plenary Commission at Lima in January 1982,
there is now presented to the churches a further document for
consideration. This document is known as *Baptism, Eucharist
and Ministry*. It is important to note that it is a convergence document not a consensus document. On some of the points
some churches will be at consensus whilst others are still on
converging paths. Each member church now has the task and the
responsibility to respond to that document. It is to be hoped
that response will not come simply from each church within a
a geographical area, but also will come from ecumenical contexts. The adverse vote on the covenant issue should spur on
Christians in England to face the questions which arise out
of this ecumenically produced document on convergence. The
failure of covenanting was due in large measure to a misappre-
hension that the churches were sufficiently close to a consensus on Ministry when, in fact, they were still in the pro-

cess of converging.   Nevertheless the call to us all is to
continue a convergence towards consensus.   Whether this new
document had to produce for us as Baptists material on
Baptism, Eucharist and Ministry which will command assent,
remains to be seen.

At Vancouver in 1983 at the Sixth World Assembly, the
Faith and Order Commission will again be reconstituted for
the next seven years.   There will be changes in Baptist representation and certainly the present writer will be retiring
from the Commission.   But the Baptist participation in Faith
and Order from 1927 to 1982 has been significant and undoubtedly has had the effect of sharing our heritage and our
understanding with others.   Without any doubt at all we must
continue to play our part as the churches under God move
towards whatever form of visible unity He wills.

NOTES

1   See E. A. Payne, *The Baptist Union: A Short History*, Carey Kingsgate
    Press, London 1959, p.177.

2   Quoted in E. A. Payne, op.cit., from W. W. Barnes, *The Southern
    Baptist Convention*, 1845-1953, pp.280-83.

3   *Faith and Order Proceedings of the World Conference, Lausanne,
    August 3-21, 1927*, ed. H. N. Bate, New York 1927, p.43.

4   ibid., p.315.

5   ibid., p.473.

6   *The Second World Conference on Faith and Order, held at Edinburgh,
    August 3-18, 1937*, ed. L. Hodgson, S.C.M.Press, London 1938, p.304.

7   *A History of the Ecumenical Movement 1517-1948*, ed. R. Rouse and
    S. C. Neill, S.P.C.K. London 1954, p.434.

8   L. Hodgson (ed.), op.cit., p.243.

9   ibid., pp.108-115.

10 ibid., p.137.

11 ibid., p.190.

12 *The Third World Conference on Faith and Order, held at Lund, August
    15th - 28th 1952*, ed. O. S. Tomkins, S.C.M.London 1953, p.16.

13 ibid., p.23.

14 ibid., p.158.

15 *Intercommunion* edited by D. Baillie and J. Marsh, S.C.M. Press, London
    1952, p.339.

16 *Faith and Order Commission Paper 17: Working Committee Minutes*,
    Bossey, August 11th - 19th 1953, p.14.

17 *Faith and Order Commission Paper 25*, Minutes of the Commission and
    the Working Committee 1957, New Haven, Connecticut, p.14.

18 ibid., pp.15-16.

19 ibid., p.18.

20 *Faith and Order Commission Paper 27*: Minutes of the Working Committee 1959, Spittal, Austria, pp.12-16.

21 ibid., p.16.

22 ibid.

23 *Faith and Order Commission Paper 31*: Minutes of the Faith and Order Commission 1960, St Andrews, Scotland, pp.49-56.

24 ibid., p.55.

25 *One Lord, One Baptism*, Faith and Order Commission Paper 29 published in series *Studies in Ministry and Worship* (No.17) ed. G. W. H. Lampe, David M. Paton, S.C.M. Press, London 1960, p.70.

26 ibid., pp.70-71.

27 Faith and Order Commission Paper 31, op.cit., pp.56-58.

28 ibid., pp.122-123.

29 *Faith and Order Findings*, Final Report of the Theological Commissions to the World Conference on Faith and Order 1963, ed. P. Minear, S.C.M. Press 1963, p.37.

30 Faith and Order Paper 50, *New Directions in Faith and Order*, Bristol 1967, p.52; see also p.119.

31 Faith and Order Paper 59, Louvain 1971, *Study Reports and Documents*, p.35 and see p.35-54.

32 op.cit., pp.49 ff.

33 Faith and Order Paper 73, *One Baptism, One Eucharist and a Mutually Recognized Ministry*.

34 ibid., p.17.

35 Faith and Order Paper 84, *Towards an Ecumenical Consensus Baptism, Eucharist, Ministry*, pp.7-8.

36 *Baptist Quarterly*, Vol.28, No.5, pp.225-232.

37 ibid., p.230.

W. M. S. WEST

BAPTISTS AND POLITICS SINCE 1914

By far the most marked feature of Baptist politics in the
twentieth century has been the decline of Liberal partisanship.
At the end of the last century a Baptist was, almost by definition, a Liberal. Under the heading "Plain politics for
plain folk", *The Freeman*, the chief Baptist weekly, compla-
cently announced in 1885, "It is a fact that under a Liberal
government the country has ever prospered more than under a
Conservative government".[1] Baptists shared with most other
Nonconformists a willingness to see the Liberal cause as their
own.[2] During the 20th century, however, there has been a
steady erosion of Liberal allegiance among Nonconformists.[3]
Already by 1929 it was possible for Stanley Baldwin, the Conservative Prime Minister, to be the guest of honour at a din-
ner held in support of the Baptist Union Superannuation Fund -
an event that would have been unthinkable to Baptists of the
previous generation.[4] Men in the denomination who had previously been life-long Liberals had voted for Baldwin's party
at the 1924 general election.[5] There were defections to the
left as well as to the right, and this tendency grew over
time. A quantitative study has recently been made of the impact of Baptists on constituency voting. It reveals that
whereas in the 1920s the Baptist effect was strongly pro-
Liberal, after the Second World War it veered more in favour
of Labour.[6] The party distribution of Baptist members of 20th
century parliaments confirms this pattern of change. Of the
23 British Baptists elected before the First World War, 20
were Liberals. None was a Conservative; only 3 represented
Labour, and all these had Liberal backgrounds. So the pre-
First World War picture is of almost total Liberal solidarity
among Baptist MPs.   In the inter-war period, there was an
almost equal three-way split: 8 sat as Liberals, 8 as Labour
men and 10 as Coalition Liberals or Liberal Nationals supporting predominantly Conservative governments.[7] In the post-war
period, Liberal MPs had entirely disappeared. There were 11
Labour MPs and 3 Conservatives. Sir Cyril Black, in 1950,
was the first Baptist ever to enter parliament as a pure Conservative.[8] Overall the pattern is one of change from Liberal
monopoly to Liberal exclusion. Although the allegiance of
ordinary Baptist voters did not alter so dramatically, the
trend was in the same direction. Liberalism among Baptists
was on the decline.

There has nevertheless been a substantial Liberal legacy
in the denomination, just as there has been in the other Free
Churches. Surveys since the Second World War have repeatedly
shown that Nonconformists have been more likely to vote Liberal than Anglicans, active or nominal, or Roman Catholics.[9]
Middle-class Nonconformists in particular have been far less
likely to be Conservative and far more likely to be Liberal
than their neighbours of other religious persuasions.[10]
Hence it is not surprising that there have been many Baptist
parliamentary candidates standing as Liberals since 1945,
even though none of them was successful. In 1945, for

instance, W. P. Hamsher, a journalist on the *News Chronicle*
who was a member of Bloomsbury Baptist Church, stood for
Acocks Green; Granville Slack, a barrister who was church secretary at Acton, contested Twickenham; R. Shackleton, origin-
ating at Wellington Road, Todmorden, fought at Blackburn; and
3 Baptists, Arnold Kirby, Wilfred Kirby and T. A. Pratt, were
defeated in Leicestershire constituencies.[11]   It has also
seemed worthwhile for Liberal leaders to appeal for Baptist
support not so much on the grounds that their party would
deliver the goods as on the grounds of an alleged affinity,
natural as well as historical, between Baptists and Liberalism. When on the eve of the 1959 general election Jo Grimond
commended Liberalism in the *Baptist Times* as "more than a
party - it is a faith", an appreciative Watford reader approved his article as "a very genuine attempt to express
Christian principles in the political field".[12]   Again, in
1982, David Steel, pointing to the symbolic significance of
the use of the disused Baptist chapel at Hebden Bridge as the
headquarters of the Association of Liberal Councillors, argued that Baptist beliefs had been "inbuilt into the Liberal
Party and its policies, often imperceptibly".[13]   At the same
period, Paul Rowntree Clifford, a Baptist who had recently
retired as president of the Selly Oak Colleges, was writing
a column headed "Politics without Apology" from time to time
in the denominational newspaper. At the 1979 election he had
stood as the Liberal candidate for Selly Oak.[14] The classless
humanitarianism of the Liberal public image, together with
its individualist, anti-bureaucratic streak, still reinforced
the inherited political leanings of many Baptists. Liberalism continued to come easily to Baptists, far more easily
than to most members of the population.

Yet the decay of party solidarity among Baptists is clearly reflected in the denomination's newspaper. At the beginning of the period the editorial policy of the *Baptist Times*
was in the hands of J. H. Shakespeare, secretary of the Baptist Union, whose brother Alfred was responsible for the day-
to-day running of the newspaper.[15]   Lloyd George, one of
whose particular skills was the management of the press, took
pains to court J. H. Shakespeare, whose assistance he invited
in dealing with the problems of the nation just before the
1918 general election and whose son Geoffrey he appointed one
of his private secretaries in 1921.[16]   Lloyd George was re-
warded with the unequivocal support of the newspaper for his
brand of Liberalism. At the 1922 election the *Baptist Times*
was the only denominational journal to give Lloyd George
wholehearted backing.[17]   In 1923 the paper rather extrava-
gantly professed to believe that Lloyd George, leading a
united Liberal Party, had eclipsed Gladstone's Midlothian
speeches with his campaign in defence of free trade.[18]   In
the following year, however, there was the first sign of
wavering in the Liberal faith. In the stampede to the right
provoked by the first Labour government, the paper declared
it would be content with a Conservative administration rely-
ing on Liberal support for a majority.[19]   Under the editor-
ship of J. C. Carlile, minister of Folkestone Baptist Church,

from 1925 to 1941, the *Baptist Times* was much more circum-
spect than under Shakespeare. At each general election the
paper endorsed no party. Yet, so far as was possible in the
circumstances, it implied a certain Liberal preference —
though in 1935 after, rather than before, the election.[20] By
1945, with Dr Townley Lord, minister of Bloomsbury, as editor,
there was no hint of partisanship; but there were no editorials
either. The only trace of residual Liberalism was to be found
in the commentary by Arthur Porritt, an elderly journalist
previously on the *Christian World*. He who could remember
every general election since 1880 could not contemplate the
"complete eclipse of the Liberal Party without sadness".[21]
He recounted with some nostalgia that a very old lady asked
where she could vote for Mr Gladstone.[22] Otherwise all evidence of Liberalism had faded from the pages.

The termination of the public identification of Baptists
with Liberalism brought with it something of a retreat from
politics in its entirety. In 1950 there was, extraordinarily,
no reference whatsoever to the general election in the issue
of the *Baptist Times* published on that very day. In the same
year the editor supposed that 4 Baptists had been elected to
parliament, whereas in fact there were 10.[23] Clearly no effort had been made to find out the true numbers. "As
churches", ran an editorial in 1951, "we do not intervene in
party political warfare".[24] In 1955 the election was editori-
ally ignored. The only signs of political awareness during
this phase were a weighty, theologically-charged article in
1951 by the rising minister of Church Road Baptist Church,
Acton, D. S. Russell, and sensible if rather bland commentary
in 1955 by Ernest Brown, the distinguished Baptist ex-cabinet
minister, by then in his seventies.[25] Baptists were increasingly distanced from political debate. The next editor of the
Baptist Times, Walter Bottoms, who took over in 1956, determined to reverse the process. He enjoyed the help of his as-
sistant editor, N. P. Thomas, who had written a history of
British politics in the first half of the century.[26] Remark-
ably, the *Baptist Times* was the only paper to publish policy
statements by the leaders of all three main political parties
in the 1959 election.[27] There were similar policy statements,
though not by party leaders, in 1964, and the practice was
revived, the leaders again contributing, in February 1974 and
1979.[28] There were inevitably protests. Criticism from Wales
led to the inclusion of Gwynfor Evans among the contributing
party leaders in 1979.[29] Correspondents from left and right
argued that their case had been misrepresented by opponents.
Another in 1959 regretted that the editor had allowed party
leaders the space "to reveal their vote-catching rubbish.
Did you pray about it before you decided to publish it?"[30]
At the same time the Christian Citizenship Department of the
Baptist Union under Clifford Cleal was trying to enhance the
denomination's sense of political responsibility. Some months
before the 1964 election, for instance, the department put out
a pamphlet, *Public Issues*.[31] There was even a resurgence of
something approaching partisanship. After the 1959, 1964 and
February 1974 elections, editorial comment, while criticising

the Conservatives and Labour, gave nothing but praise to the
Liberals. [32] In 1970 the message of a pre-election editorial,
implicit rather than explicit, was pro-Liberal; the same was
true of comment on the day of the October 1974 election. [33]
Again there were protests. In 1964, for instance, a retired
lieutenant-colonel from Herne Bay condemned the "obvious party political bias" against the Conservatives. [34] Nevertheless
it seems probable that Baptists contributed in a small way
to the improvement in the fortunes of the Liberals that
marked the 1960s and 1970s: there is evidence that middle-
class Nonconformists in general were much more likely to vote
Liberal than they had been in the previous two decades. [35]
Certainly the *Baptist Times* reflected a rather higher degree
of interest in public affairs in the 1960s and 1970s. Before
that time most political issues were hot potatoes in a denomination divided by party, and so they tended to be dropped.
By the 1960s Baptists were learning how to deal with political questions in a non-contentious way. They were coming to
terms with the experience of being politically divided.

Why did the long-term erosion of Baptist identification
with Liberalism take place? It is fundamentally to be explained as a decay of communal politics. In the late 19th
century, political parties normally drew bloc support from
communities like churches and chapels rather than from classes. As the century wore on, the disabilities that had
driven Nonconformists to support the Liberal Party were
steadily removed. The original reason for Baptists being
Liberals was therefore disappearing. By the first decade of
the 20th century many Baptists might feel that the grievances
that had spurred their fathers into Liberalism had gone entirely, except in the field of education. The chapel communities had less intrinsic cause to be partisan. For a
while this reality was obscured by the force of tradition,
but by the 1920s tradition was no longer sufficient to ensure
Liberal solidarity in the chapels. At the same time their
social cohesion was weakening. There was less commitment to
the chapels as alternative outlets for leisure time multi-
plied - organised sport, clubs and cinemas, and later radio,
television and cars. Businessmen were less likely to expect
chapel-going from their employees as family firms gave way to
larger industrial units. Greater mobility, geographical and
social, accentuated the change. Families uprooted from their
original homes often weakened in their denominational allegiance; others rose beyond the social milieu that they associated with Baptists. As the social bonds of the chapels
weakened in the early 20th century, political choice was decreasingly likely to be determined by churchmanship. Even if
a person remained a loyal Baptist, his other social ties were
increasingly likely to sway his vote. In particular, the
economic interests of his social group would influence his
party allegiance. Communal politics was giving way to class
politics. Negatively, this meant that the traditional sanction for voting Liberal was undermined; positively, it meant
that the attractions of the Conservatives and Labour, the
parties standing for the interests of the two great social
classes, were enhanced. As the two main parties became orga-

nised nationally, even local government in the countryside
became a battleground for class issues rather than a competition between church and chapel.[36]   The Liberalism of Baptists
was sapped by the social changes that impinged on their chapels.

The process was accelerated by political circumstances.
Liberalism between the wars had a strange urge to self-destruc-
tion, much of the impetus coming from the convoluted manoeuvres
of that practising but insincere Baptist, Lloyd George. The
decision of Lloyd George as wartime Prime Minister of a coalition government to go to the country in 1918 still in alliance with the Conservatives drove a sharp wedge into Baptist
political solidarity. "Liberals will find themselves in a
very awkward position", commented a Baptist MP. "While they
may be prepared to support Mr Lloyd George, they cannot blind
themselves to the fact that the present Government is predominantly Tory".[37] Some followed the *Baptist Times* in backing
Lloyd George; others preferred to vote for opposition Liberal
or Labour candidates. Among the latter were members of the
committee of the Yorkshire Baptist Association which formally
resolved its dismay at the support of the *Baptist Times* for
Lloyd George's coalition.[38] John Clifford, the veteran Baptist leader, chaired a Nonconformist rally in favour of the
Labour programme, drawing other eminent Baptists like Charles
Brown, Thomas Phillips, J. H. Rushbrooke and F. C. Spurr to
his side.[39] With the Liberal split persisting in 1922, Baptists were again compelled to stand either for or against
Lloyd George's alliance between Liberals and Conservatives.
T. R. Glover, the distinguished Cambridge scholar, was one
of those who refused to follow Lloyd George.[40] Although the
breach was healed in 1923, Baptists again divided into friends
and opponents of Lloyd George during the wrangles of the later
1920s and the early 1930s.[41] A similar though different
choice was presented in the later 1930s: either to adhere to
those Liberals who, like Ernest Brown, supported the National
government and became decreasingly distinguishable from moderate Conservatives; or to identify with the rump of the Liberals who remained outside the government.[42] In such circumstances, a united front in party political terms was an im-
possibility for Baptists, even had they wished to adopt one.
And perhaps most adverse of all to continued Liberal allegiance was the absence of Liberal candidates to vote for. At
the 1945 election, for example, less than half the constituencies had a Liberal candidate.[43] Would-be Liberals were
forced either to abstain or to vote for the representative of
another party and so acquire a taste for a different political
menu. The remarkable disarray of the Liberal Party was as
damaging among Baptists as it was in other sections of the
population.

In a few parts of the country, communal politics has sur-
vived the vicissitudes of the twentieth century to a remarkable
degree. In the remote fenland, for example, Baptist small-
holders are still the backbone of Liberalism in Clement Freud's
constituency of the Isle of Ely. But the best cases of the
perpetuation of chapel influence in politics far into the 20th
century are to be found in Wales. With fewer alternative

leisure activities than in some other parts and little inward
population movement, many of the chapels have continued to be
both relatively tightly knit and among the chief centres of
social life. It long remained customary for the leading
figures of the chapels to dominate local political affairs,
which in consequence were strongly coloured by religion. As
recently as 1950 a proposal to open meetings of Neath Rural
District Council with prayer was rejected by only fourteen
votes to eight.[44] In the next year in the area round Swansea,
12.8% of office-holders in Baptist chapels and Sunday schools
were found to be active in a political party or local government.[45] In most of Wales, however, there has been a realign-
ment of political allegiance. In the years following the
First World War, with apparently nothing more to be gained
from the Liberals after the passing of Welsh disestablishment,
Nonconformists in Wales commonly transferred their loyalty to
Labour.[46] The Labour Party recruited strongly in Nonconformity. Of 175 Labour Party officials in the Swansea area in
1951, 40 held office in the chapels.[47] This has been reflected very strikingly among 20th century Baptist MPs. Of the
17 who have represented Labour, no fewer than 14 have been
Welsh.[48] They have been the representatives of a culture
where politics and religion have been as closely intertwined
as in late 19th century England. More recently Plaid Cymru
has drawn strongly on the chapels, especially in the rural
and Welsh-speaking west.[49] The first president of Plaid was
a Baptist minister, Lewis Valentine, and a principal of Ban-
gor Baptist College, David Eirwyn Morgan, stood for parliament three times as a Plaid candidate.[50] The association is
natural: the cultural forces undermining the social central-
ity of the chapels come from England on the English-speaking
media. The defence of the chapels seems to entail a defence
of Welshness. Although in some parts of Wales, Liberalism
is still the natural vehicle for the political expression of
Baptist life, it is not generally so. Even when the bond
with Liberalism has been snapped, however, politics has remained far more of a communal affair than in all but the re-
motest corners of England.

     It is clear that the deep-seated and external factors
making for the waning of communal politics have been supple-
mented by more conscious decisions to edge away from politics.
The withdrawal from political engagement evident in the
Baptist Times around mid-century was partly the result of
pragmatic choice. Baptist churches were smaller in attendance and membership. Hence there was a psychology of withdrawal, a sense that the Baptist house must be put in order
before the nation's life could be swept clean. Furthermore,
as the 20th century advanced, the state grew bigger, taking
an increasing responsibility for the wellbeing of the people
and intervening more firmly in economic affairs. With the
emergence of the welfare state and the managed economy after
the Second World War, it seemed that Christian influence was
far less likely to impinge on policy-making. What has been
called the "corporate bias" of the British state, its willingness to take organisations representing workers and em-

ployers into permanent, institutionalised consultation, has
had the effect of excluding other pressure groups like the
churches from the centres of power.[51] Hence there has been a
strong disincentive to political activity by Christians either
as individuals or as churches. David might take on Goliath,
but Goliath would always win.

Alongside these pragmatic reasons for withdrawal from politics there have been inhibiting theological attitudes. Traditional Calvinism was a restraint on the theologically most
conservative among Baptists. The ministry of J. K. Popham,
for 55 years pastor of Galeed Strict Baptist Chapel, Brighton,
and editor of *The Gospel Standard* from 1905 to 1936, was,
according to his biographer, "eminently spiritual and never
intermixed with political and other topics". Yet he did find
time to lead his congregation in protesting when, in 1929, the
King sent a congratulatory message to the Pope. This was because, again in the words of his biographer, "loyalty to the
throne, and Protestantism of a vigorous if not militant type,
characterized Mr Popham's attitude towards politics".[52] Such
views were not confined to Strict Baptists for they approxi-
mated to the political position of Spurgeon in his last years,[53]
and Spurgeon wielded a mighty sway over innumerable Baptists
in the first half of the 20th century. Newer theological
attitudes, however, probably did more to discourage political
activity. For those who fell under the spell of Keswick
teaching about the possibilities of the higher spiritual life,
politics could seem a worldly distraction. This was not necessarily so: a Stirlingshire Baptist minister, William Wright,
for example, was a dedicated exponent of Keswick ideas, yet
accepted nomination as an independent Liberal candidate at the
1922 election.[54] But it is noteworthy that F. B. Meyer, the
chief Baptist figure in the Keswick movement, retreated sharply
from political activity after wholehearted participation in the
Free Church campaign against the Education Act of 1902. He
decided to leave socio-political issues to others: he would
concentrate on the spiritual.[55] In Britain, as in America,
there seems to have been a reaction among Evangelical Christians, especially those influenced by Keswick, against socio-
political work because of its association with liberal theology.[56] Certainly the spread of premillennial ideas, which
among Baptists owed much to permeation by ex-Christian Brethren and the use of the Scofield Bible, as well as to Meyer's
Advent Testimony and Preparation Movement, helped to dissoci-
ate politics from religion. "Personally", wrote a premillen-
ial correspondent to the *Baptist Times* in 1950, "I doubt the
propriety of Christians taking any part either in voting or
taking office in government, local or national... Christians
should regard themselves as citizens of a Kingdom of a far
higher order... to be revealed... in the personal return of
Jesus...".[57] A few years before the Second World War another
premillenialist had objected to church advocacy of peace
through the League of Nations on the ground that this was to
fly in the face of Christ's prophecy of wars shortly before
his return.[58] The underswell of this popular theology should
not be underestimated. It was a potent force discouraging all

political activity, and left-of-centre activity in particular.
M. E. Aubrey, secretary of the Baptist Union from 1925 to
1951, seems to have been swayed by both pragmatic and theological considerations to steer the denomination away from the
degree of political involvement that had marked the term of
office of J. H. Shakespeare. Aubrey assumed office as something of a protégé of T. R. Glover, one of his deacons at St
Andrew's Street, Cambridge, who, as president of the Union in
1924, achieved "the settlement of the secretariat".[59]   Glover
had been sternly opposed to Shakespeare's publicly partisan
stance and Aubrey was no doubt influenced by his mentor.[60]
Aubrey's own political views are elusive. Only occasionally
is there a glimmer of light, as when he wrote in 1931 that
the Labour scheme for nationalising banks was playing with
fire, and so "wholly mischievous".[61]   His attitudes became
clearest at the time of the Council of Action in 1935. This
was essentially a project devised by the ageing Lloyd George
for securing greater political leverage through persuading
the Free Churches, and anyone else who could be drummed in,
to agitate for peace and increased public spending. He swept
in many Methodists under Scott Lidgett, many Congregationalists
under Sidney Berry and, among Baptists, Robert Wilson Black,
Charles Brown and S. W. Hughes, secretary of the National
Free Church Council. Aubrey refused to participate, resigning
from the Free Church Council executive when it endorsed the
Council of Action. He argued pragmatically that the failure
of Nonconformists to benefit from their efforts on behalf of
the Liberals at the 1906 election showed the ineffectiveness
of Free Church political pressure. He may well have been
counselled against involvement by Ernest Brown, a member of
the Baptist Union Council who, as a new cabinet member, perceived that Lloyd George was executing an anti-government
manoeuvre. But it seems clear that he objected to politicking
chiefly because he saw it as a threat to the spirituality of
the church. He protested against "the Church of God, or any
part of it, being dragged through the mire of an electioneer-
ing campaign".[62] Aubrey was quite prepared to tolerate public
resolutions by the Union - they were frequent in his time -
but was extremely wary of doing more to sway national policy.
He helped to create the apolitical tone of Baptist life around
mid-century.

    If there were pressures tending to draw Baptists away from
the political fray, there were some public issues in every
decade that encouraged them to re-enter the arena. The question of peace was prominent among them. After the First World
War, hopes of a new and harmonious world order rested on the
League of Nations. Sir William Beddoe Rees, a Welsh coalowner,
a Liberal MP and a member of the Tredegarville Church, Cardiff,
was one of many Baptists who spoke for the League of Nations
Union;[63] Baptist churches commonly affiliated to the Union as
corporate members;[64] and associations passed resolutions in
favour of the League.[65] The long established Peace Society,
despite having a Baptist minister and later Labour MP, Herbert
Dunnico, as its secretary, was too much of a fading force to

attract much Baptist support.[66]   Even those opposed to all war
put their faith in the League.[67]   Of these there were relatively few in the Baptist ranks.   The denomination had contributed
its fair share of conscientious objectors in the Great War
(almost certainly proportionately more than the Methodists),[68]
but only in Wales had pacifism struck deep root.[69]   One Welsh
Baptist, Morgan Jones, was the first conscientious objector
to be returned to parliament, in 1921.[70]   In 1933 the Welsh
Baptist Union passed a pacifist resolution and urged the Baptist Union of Great Britain and Ireland to do the same.   A
committee of the Union reported in 1936 that the best avenue
to world peace lay in the abolition of the notion of national
sovereignty.[71]   The Baptist Pacifist Fellowship had been set
up two years earlier through the efforts of W. H. Haden, minister of Salem, Burton-on-Trent, to stand for the absolutist
position.[72]   The Fellowship continued after the Second World
War, but the revulsion against the appeasement of the 1930s
meant that the quest for peace loomed far less large on Baptist
horizons in the post-war world.   Voices were raised against the
arms trade, the independent nuclear deterrent and the Vietnam
war,[73]   but they rarely found a wide audience.   A concern for
peace had roused more interest in public affairs during the
inter-war years.

By contrast the other international issue to stir Baptists,
the protection of religious minorities from oppression, commanded more attention after the Second World War.   Between
the wars the personal representations of J. H. Rushbrooke on
behalf of the Baptist World Alliance did a great deal to alle-
viate the plight of foreign Baptists harassed for their faith,
especially in Rumania, but his diplomacy was usually behind
closed doors.[74]   The sufferings of Baptists in Russia, though
acute after 1929, were relatively little known.   Geoffrey
Shakespeare asked the Foreign Office to try to shield them
from Communist persecution, just as his father had tried to
protect them from Tsarist persecution years before, but to no
avail.[75]   After the war, popular anti-Communism made concern
for Christians in Eastern Europe far more widespread, though
much less sensitive to the issues involved.   A few Baptists,
among whom Dr E. A. Payne and Dr D. S. Russell were the chief,
were able to make representations on behalf of religious minorities abroad.   When Dr Payne, with Dr Townley Lord and the
B.W.A. secretary, visited Russia in 1954 to make contact with
Baptists, they also had a useful interview with the state official in charge of religious affairs.[76]   Dr Payne's preoccu-
pation with oppression abroad led him to be one of the founders
of Amnesty International in 1961, and, more controversially,
to defend the decision of the World Council of Churches to make
grants for humanitarian purposes to African guerilla organisations.[77]   But the outstanding case of Baptist concern about
oppression abroad was the remarkable outburst of protest over
Angola in 1961.   The Portuguese regime of Dr Salazar had long
harboured suspicions that the Protestant missionaries in Angola,
including those of the B.M.S., were sowing the seeds of revolu-
tion against its colonial rule.   The B.M.S. had in fact scrupu-
lously avoided political issues, although its educational work

was training a generation of Angolans capable of expressing
the rising national feeling in the country. When in March
1961 rebellion broke out in northern Angola and Portuguese
settlers were massacred, the authorities replied with a campaign of unbridled ferocity that was directed particularly at
Africans associated with Protestant missions.[78] Early reports
induced the B.M.S., with the aid of the Baptist Labour MP
Clifford Kenyon, to seek Foreign Office assistance in pressing
the Portuguese for restraint, but the government was reluctant
to embarrass a N.A.T.O. ally.[79] Two Baptist ministers in
Southend, Len Addicott and Eric Blakeborough, decided that
only a mass agitation would modify government policy, and so
spent a couple of frenetic months in making contacts, securing
publicity and issuing information gathered from missionaries.
Their "Angola Action Group" faced opposition, not least in
their own Essex Baptist Association, but they received encour-
agement from Dr Payne and J. B. Middlebrook, secretary of the
B.M.S.[80] It was very much a Baptist-spearheaded operation,
with such incidents as a Baptist minister, Walter Bailey,
setting out to walk barefoot from Stoke-on-Trent to Westminster and Viscount Alexander of Hillsborough putting a crucial
question in the Lords.[81] On the day that George Thomas, the
Methodist MP and later Speaker, presented a petition to the
Commons, it was announced that Britain had suspended arms
supplies to Portuguese overseas territories, a significant
signal of British disquiet.[82] World opinion was alerted and
repression in Angola may well have been mitigated. Baptists
showed that they could be roused in defence of religious
liberty to mass protest.

There were also domestic issues that pulled Baptists towards the political sphere. Baptists never systematised their
attitudes to social questions, as did the Methodists.[83] Their
representatives did participate in church conferences on such
matters, of which the most significant was C.O.P.E.C. (the
Conference on Politics, Economics and Citizenship) in 1924,
but they were less prominent than figures from other denominations like William Temple for the Church of England and
Principal A. E. Garvie for Congregationalism. It is true that
a Baptist, Hugh Martin, was chairman of the executive of
C.O.P.E.C., but otherwise the only Baptist contribution was
a statement by Alexander Graham-Barton, minister of the de-
clining Kingsgate Church, about general political responsibility.[84] Industrial problems tended to be neglected by Baptists, as any comment at all could be construed as politically
partisan. Even in the general strike of 1926, whose opening
coincided with the Baptist Union assembly, a group of ministers who tried to put together some Christian policy abandoned the task as fruitless.[85] One of the few who seized the
opportunity was J. N. Britton of the Avenue Church, Southend-
on-Sea, who addressed a packed congregation on "What shall it
profit a man if he gain the whole world and lose his own soul?"[86]
It was he again who delivered a telling address on "Industri-
alism" to the Toronto Congress of the Baptist World Alliance
in 1928.[87] Unemployment was lamented and the unemployed often
given personal relief, but little more seemed practical. Only

Ernest Brown, as Minister of Labour from 1935 to 1940, was in a position to act; he personally supervised the revision of unemployment relief regulations, and was able to redirect government contracts to areas where work was scarce.[88]   Slum clearance was endorsed by association resolutions,[89]   but again it was a government minister, Geoffrey Shakespeare, who had the power to act. As Parliamentary Secretary to the Ministry of Health from 1932 to 1936, he prodded local authorities into extensive clearance of unsatisfactory housing.[90] The social questions of the day did attract Baptist attention, but their communal voice was muted by the complexity of the issues and their own sense of impotence.

There was, however, a set of social issues over which Baptists felt and often spoke intensely. These were the problems which, unlike unemployment or housing, could be analysed in terms of personal responsibility. In drunkenness, Sunday desecration and gambling, Baptists held, there was something condemned by the Bible and therefore decisively wrong. Temperance feeling was stronger in the denomination in the first half of the 20th century than in the second half of the 19th. Government restrictions on drink outlets during the First World War, the example of the King's pledge to total abstinence and the precedent of prohibition in the United States conspired to raise hopes of effective legislation against alcohol. In 1929 an article in the *Baptist Times* gave as its sole reason for backing the Liberals the fact that they alone had a temperance policy.[91]   The chief thrust of Baptist Union official social concern was over temperance. In 1926 it took over the work of the formerly independent Baptist Total Abstinence Association and in the following year all temperance, social work and youth matters were entrusted to Dr T. G. Dunning.[92]   The focal point of his interests is indicated by his destination when he left the service of the Union: in 1952 he became secretary of the Temperance Council of the Christian Churches.[93]   Robert Wilson Black, perhaps the leading Baptist layman of his day, was president of the United Kingdom Alliance from 1932 until his death in 1951.[94]   One of his greatest achievements was the healing, in 1933, of a long-standing split between the prohibitionist Alliance and those who advocated public ownership of drink outlets.[95]   Thereafter temperance forces were united in their desire for a string of measures that commanded the general support of Baptists. Zeal for reforms in this area was perceptibly abating in the early 1950s, as Robert Wilson Black's son Cyril lamented,[96]   but at that time the young people of Scarborough Baptist Church could still take a spontaneous part in opposing a dance hall licence.[97] Opposition to Sunday desecration came second to temperance on the socio-political agenda for Baptists. The only observation ventured by Aubrey at the 1929 election was to hope that no Baptist would support a candidate who attended a Sunday political meeting.[98] The threat of Sunday opening of theatres and cinemas was acutely felt in the 1940s and 1950s.[99]   The strongest feeling about such intrusions on the sabbath was aroused in the least secularised area, Wales. A Nonconformist-influenced newspaper commented, when in 1939 Welsh nationalists

set fire to the Lleyn bombing school, that bombing ought not
to take place on Sundays.[100]   There was vigorous campaigning
by the chapels to keep their counties dry on Sundays in local
polls in 1961 and 1968.[101]   A cause that blended temperance
and sabbatarian principles was deeply stirring. Gambling was
the third target in a trinity of sin. Greyhound racing and
the growth of football pools were deplored in the inter-war
period,[102] but feeling was at its strongest against the public sanction given to gambling by the introduction of Premium
Bonds in 1957. Several correspondents of the *Baptist Times*
at the 1959 election wondered whether that should determine
their vote.[103]   These were the domestic issues that were most
likely to rouse Baptists from political apathy. None seemed
a progressive cause, at least after America dropped prohibition, and concern with such matters has undoubtedly acted as
a brake on potential Christian support for Labour.[104]   Defence
of moral causes by Baptists has tended to swing them to the
right.

The "permissive society" of the 1960s and 1970s presented
Baptists with a new moral challenge. Could they tolerate the
liberalisation of the law on such matters as homosexual relations and abortion? Like most denominations, they were re-
markably quiescent, no doubt partly for fear of being branded
as unprogressive, but also because a minority in their ranks
saw at least some of the legal changes as sensible. One minister called in 1966 for homosexuals to be treated as psycho-
logically ill and therefore not subject to the criminal law.[105]
Yet the majority view was that the relaxation of legal standards was a retreat from Christian values. David Steel and
the Liberal Party still suffered from his association with
the 1967 abortion law reform fifteen years after the event.[106]
Sexual explicitness, and especially pornography, formed a
newly obtrusive sin in Baptist eyes. Hence Baptists rallied
to support the Festival of Light, an attempt to organise
opposition to "moral pollution" that was launched in 1971
with a series of beacons up and down the country.[107]   Five
years later the organisation held a commemorative gathering
in Trafalgar Square at which denominational affiliation was
measured. 42% of attenders were Anglican, 22% were Baptist
and (next largest) 9% were Pentecostal or charismatic.[108]
Baptist backing was disproportionately high. Their share in
the Festival of Light has further significance. The groups
supporting the Festival were primarily, though not entirely,
from what had until recently been called the "conservative
Evangelical" camp, but was increasingly labelled simply
"Evangelical". 41% of the attenders at Trafalgar Square said
that evangelistic concern was the chief reason for their
presence; only 3.5% were primarily wanting legislation against
immorality.[109]   Most Baptists by the 1970s found their natural
home here. Rather than co-operating with Nonconformists of
all theological types in activities more or less in rivalry
with the Church of England, they stood alongside Evangelical
Anglicans in a protest against secular trends. Some denominations had increasingly adapted themselves to a secularising
culture; rank-and-file Baptists instinctively joined like-

minded Christians in opposing the tendencies of the day.
Baptists were choosing the path of resistance to secularisa-
tion rather than that of accommodation.[110]   That course, set
in the 1970s, seemed likely to bring them, in due time, into
greater tension with authorities in the state.

   If the gravity of some social problems drew Baptists towards
politics, the easing of ecclesiastical problems was another of
the factors that allowed them to distance themselves from the
political process. As the ecumenical movement drew the churches closer together, old quarrels that had spilled over into
the political arena were steadily made up. The campaign for
the disestablishment of the Church of England generated only
a tiny head of steam in the 20th century - apart from in Wales
in its first two decades. Wilson Black was one of the few
Baptists to treat the cause seriously, becoming in 1945 trea-
surer of the Liberation Society that aimed for disestablishment. Dr Henry Townsend, principal of Manchester Baptist College, became its president in the same year.[111]   Aubrey had
told the Royal Commission on Church and State which reported
in 1935 that Free Churchmen still believed the establishment
principle wrong, but that they looked for its voluntary renunciation by Anglicans themselves.[112]   Dr Payne similarly held
the unique state recognition of the Church of England to be
unjustified, but explicitly rejected the desirability of the
Free Churches pressing for disestablishment.[113]   In 1959 Dr
Payne took the lead in dissolving the Liberation Society altogether when it seemed likely to fall under the control of a
historian who wished to revive its 19th century glories. Consequently it was the education issue that formed the nub of
political debate between the churches in the 20th century.
The essential aim of the Free Churches, as it had been since
1870, was to eliminate or at least minimise the advantages
enjoyed by other churches in state-supported education. The
Church of England still provided the only school in many parts
of the country, so that the children of Nonconformists had to
accept Anglican instruction or else be conspicuous by with-
drawing under the "conscience clause".[114]   Furthermore, the
Church of England was not the only ecclesiastical body in the
field of education: there were also Roman Catholic schools.
Nonconformist suspicion of Rome and the Romanising party in
Anglicanism was allayed far later than resentment of the pri-
vileges of the Church of England as an institution. Anti-
Catholicism was a powerful current in Baptist attitudes, sur-
facing, for instance, in condemnation of the Revised Prayer
Book of 1927 as disloyal to the Reformation. The MP whose
"ultra-Protestant harangue" ensured its rejection by the Commons, Rosslyn Mitchell, though not baptised as a believer,[115]
had been associated with Hillhead Baptist Church, Glasgow.
Relations with the Roman Catholic Church were hardly sweetened
at all until after the Second Vatican Council. Since Roman
Catholics were pressing for increased state subsidies for
their schools, Baptists felt bound to resist.

   There were three occasions when the churches and the state
engaged in extended negotiations leading to Education Acts -
those of 1936, 1944 and 1959. Nonconformist involvement,

which was channelled through the Free Church Council, was decreasingly effective over time.   In the discussions leading to the 1936 act, the Nonconformist position was strengthened by coinciding with that of the National Union of Teachers, which disliked the tests imposed on staff in church schools, and by the reluctance of the National government to risk provoking an education controversy like that in the first decade of the century.   Accordingly only limited concessions were made to the the Anglicans and Catholics.[116]   The main plank of R. A. Butler's solution to the religious difficulty in the 1944 act was very welcome to Nonconformists.   It was the distinction between voluntary aided church schools, receiving less public money for capital expenditure but largely independent, and controlled church schools, receiving more money but under public supervision.[117]   The removal of compulsion for church schools in single-school areas to become controlled, however, represented a reverse for the Free Churches during negotiations.   Dr Scott Lidgett, the veteran Methodist education specialist, was prepared to give much more ground than the chief Baptist representatives, Wilson Black and Henry Townsend, and Lidgett's view prevailed.[118]   Since Roman Catholics felt unable to accept controlled status for their schools, they pressed during the 1950s for more generous terms for vóluntary aided schools.   In the 1959 act they secured much of what they wanted.   It was a battle which, as Dr Payne admitted, the Free Churches lost.   The Free Church Federal Council Education Committee was no longer active, and so the Nonconformist case was ill prepared; Free Church MPs proved unreliable; and the minister in charge, Geoffrey Lloyd, was able to pose as a mediator between the Nonconformists and the Anglicans, and so impose his own terms.[119]   But the fundamental explanation was that increased grants to church schools now aroused little passion amongst Nonconformists.[120]   There was a disinclination to fight political battles over differences that were fitter for discussion round the table of an inter-denominational committee; and Baptists were soon beginning to show a preference for sending their own children to Anglican schools rather than to schools impregnated with secular values.   When state grants to church schools were improved again in 1967, there was scarcely any opposition.[121] With education ceasing to be a matter of inter-church controversy, the chief reason for political pressure exerted against other Christians disappeared.

    Baptist political activity in the 20th century therefore presents a kaleidoscopic picture.   The inherited structure of communal politics, in which Baptists automatically voted Liberal, was transformed by a turn of the kaleidoscope into a far more complex pattern.   Baptists became supporters of all three main parties - and of the Nationalists, too.   The diminution of the Baptist constituency and the extension of the sphere of the state encouraged withdrawal from politics altogether; so did widespread theological attitudes.   A number of public issues, international and domestic, pushed Baptists back into pressure-group politics, although the decay of inter-church rivalry made the most important pressure-group

role of Nonconformists before the First World War, in the
field of education, increasingly redundant. Underlying nearly
all the changes, however, was a thread of continuity: content-
ment with the structure of the state. Dr Russell voiced a
widespread conviction when he declared in 1951 that the right
to vote in Britain is an expression of the freedom Baptists
had fought to achieve.[122]   Only one feature of the political
system attracted a significant degree of Baptist criticism,
the first-past-the-post method of election. This method, according to a persistent critic, John Ivory Cripps, the West
Midland area superintendent, was "a roaring farce", since
party representation in parliament bore no resemblance to
voting strength in the country. It was "the bounden duty" of
Christians to agitate for proportional representation, or at
least a second ballot or alternative vote system.[123]   The outstanding losers under the existing electoral system have been
the Liberals, and it is noteworthy that the stream of calls
for proportional representation dried up after 1945, by which
time the Liberalism of the denomination was in decay. This
form of criticism apart, there was a chorus of praise for
parliament, freedom and democracy. An address by Ernest Brown
to the Copenhagen Baptist World Congress in 1947 was typical.
"We Baptists", he announced, "are passionate supporters of
free democracy, for it is evangelical in its essence and its
motive-power is love of God and our neighbours".[124]   After
Aubrey had expressed very similar views to the previous Baptist
World Congress at Atlanta in 1939, however, the next speaker
took him to task for confusing Christian ideals with political
ideology. The speaker, Paul Schmidt, from Berlin, argued that
Baptists were bound to no form of political life and must loy-
ally accept any government, whether collectivist or liberal-
democratic.[125]   This attitude did not wither on the collapse
of the Third Reich. At a Consultation of National Baptist
Unions of Socialist Countries held in Moscow in 1979, A. M.
Bichkov, secretary of the Russian Union, praised socialist
society for meeting the needs of people according to their
work and argued that Christians must always be "model citizens".
This view, of course, would not be echoed by Georgi Vins.
Yet it remains true that Baptists in so-called totalitarian
states have frequently discerned merits in their systems, and
have generally regarded it as their duty not to reform but
obey. The assumption that liberal democracy is somehow dis-
tinctively Christian has not been shared by all Baptists.
As Christian values ebb away in public life, an increasingly
secular liberal democracy of the future might give less satis-
faction to Baptists in Britain. But it remains true that for
most of the 20th century, while British Baptists were ceasing
to be predominantly Liberal in the narrow, party-political
sense, they were emphatically liberal in the broader, politi-
cal-theory sense of being warmly attached to the system of
liberal democracy.

NOTES

1 *Freeman*, 6 Nov.1885, p.752.

2 D. W. Bebbington, *The Nonconformist Conscience; chapel and politics, 1870-1914*, London, 1982, pp.7-11.

3 David Butler and Donald Stokes, *Political Change in Britain; forces shaping electoral choice*, Harmondsworth, 1971, p.170.

4 *Baptist Times*, 31 Jan. 1929, pp.76 f. J. C. Carlile, *My Life's Little Day*, London, 1935, p.170.

5 *Baptist Times*, 7 Nov.1924, p.726.

6 Multiple regression techniques are used to isolate the electoral effect of Baptists in relation to Anglicans. The method of assessing the number of Baptist voters is rather clumsy, but this objection should not invalidate the general trend. W. L. Miller, *Electoral Dynamics in Britain since 1918*, London, 1977, p.177.

7 Of the eight Liberals, four subsequently took the Coalition Liberal or Liberal National whip. These have here been counted twice.

8 Sir Herbert Butcher was elected in 1937 as a Liberal National, first standing as a National Liberal and Conservative in 1950. Full details on 20th century Baptist MPs are to appear in an article in *The Baptist Quarterly*.

9 A. H. Birch, *Small-Town Politics: a study of political life in Glossop*, London, 1959, p.112. Frank Bealey, Jean Blondel and W. P. McCann, *Constituency Politics: a study of Newcastle-under-Lyme*, London, 1965, p.257. P. J. Madgwick, Non Griffiths and Valerie Walker, *The Politics of Rural Wales: a study of Cardiganshire*, London, 1973, p. 80.

10 W. L. Miller and Gillian Raab, 'The Religious Alignment at English Elections between 1918 and 1970', *Political Studies*, 25, 1977, p.231.

11 *Baptist Times*, 14 Jun.1945, p.5; 21 Jun.1945, p.5; 28 Jun.1945, p.5.

12 *Baptist Times*, 1 Oct.1959, p.1; E. F. Story to editor, 8 Oct.1959, p.6.

13 *Baptist Times*, 15 Apr.1982, p.5.

14 *Baptist Times*, 26 Apr.1979, p.4. He also publicly defended the policies of the alliance between the Liberals and the newly launched Social Democratic Party. *The Times*, 5 Dec.1981, p.71.

15 E. A. Payne, *The Baptist Union: a short history*, London, 1958, p.195.

16 D. Lloyd George to editor, 19 Nov.1918, *Baptist Times*, 13 Dec.1918, p.742. Sir Geoffrey Shakespeare, *Let Candles be brought in*, London, 1949, p.37. Cf. the essay in this volume by R. Hayden, "Still at the Cross Roads? J. H. Shakespeare and Ecumenism", p.

17 Stephen Koss, *Nonconformity in Modern British Politics*, London, 1975, p.164.

18 *Baptist Times*, 7 Dec.1923, p.845.

19 *Baptist Times*, 24 Oct. 1924, p.694.

20 *Baptist Times*, 16 May 1929, p.379; 29 Oct.1931, p.763; 21 Nov.1935, p.851.

21 *Baptist Times*, 5 Jul.1945, p.2; 2 Aug.1945, p.2.

22 *Baptist Times*, 12 Jul.1945, p.2.

102.5

23 *Baptist Times*, 2 Mar.1950, p.8.

24 *Baptist Times*, 1 Nov.1951, p.7.

25 *Baptist Times*, 18 Oct.1951, p.7; 2 Jun.1955, p.3.

26 N. P. Thomas, *A History of British Politics from the Year 1900*, London, 1956.

27 *Baptist Times*, 17 Sep.1959, pp.1, 3; 24 Sep.1959, pp.1f.; 1 Oct.1959, pp.1f., 4.

28 *Baptist Times*, 24 Sep.1964, p.9; 1 Oct.1964, p.9; 8 Oct.1964, p.9; 3 Oct. 1974, pp.6f.; 19 Apr.1979, pp.4f.

29 H. S. Price to editor, *Baptist Times*, 17 Oct.1974, p.5.

30 G. H. Elvin to editor, *Baptist Times*, 1 Oct.1959, p.6.

31 *Baptist Times*, 10 Sep.1964, p.5.

32 *Baptist Times*, 15 Oct.1959, p.2; 22 Oct.1964, p.5; 28 Feb.1974, p.1.

33 *Baptist Times*, 4 Jun.1970, p.5; 10 Oct.1974, p.1.

34 Lt.-Col. E. C. Dupont to editor, *Baptist Times*, 24 Sep.1964, p.4.

35 Miller and Raab, 'Religious Alignment', *Political Studies*, 25, 1977, p.236.

36 J. F. Glaser, 'English Nonconformity and the Decline of Liberalism', *American Historical Review*, 63, 1958. P. F. Clarke, 'Electoral Sociology of Modern Britain', *History*, 57, 1972. R. W. Johnson, 'The Nationalisation of English Rural Politics: Norfolk South West, 1945-1970', *Parliamentary Affairs*, 26, 1972.

37 *Baptist Times*, 8 Nov.1918, p.664. 'A Baptist MP' had contributed a weekly article for nearly nine years.

38 *Baptist Times*, 13 Dec.1918, p.748.

39 *Baptist Times*, 13 Dec.1918, p.767.

40 T. R. Glover to editor, *Baptist Times*, 3 Nov.1922, p.115.

41 E.g. *Baptist Times*, 22 Oct.1931, p.743.

42 E.g. *Baptist Times*, 7 Nov.1935, p.811.

43 Paul Addison, *The Road to 1945: British politics and the Second World War*, London, 1975, p.264.

44 Tom Brennan, E. W. Cooney and Harold Pollins, *Social Change in South-West Wales*, London, 1954, p.157. I am grateful to Prof. K. N. Medhurst for this reference and for other suggestions in relation to this article.

45 Ibid., p.127.

46 K. O. Morgan, *Rebirth of a Nation: Wales, 1880-1980*, Oxford, 1981, p.193.

47 Brennan, Cooney and Pollins, *Social Change*, p.157.

48 Cf. forthcoming article in *The Baptist Quarterly* on 20th century Baptist MPs.

49 Brennan, Cooney and Pollins, *Social Change*, p.137. Madgwick, Griffiths and Walker, *Politics of Rural Wales*, p.80.

50 *Baptist Times*, 7 Mar.1974, p.12.

51 Keith Middlemas, *Politics in Industrial Society: the experience of the British system since 1911*, London, 1979, pp.373 f.

52 J. H. Gosden, *Memoir and Letters of James Kidwell Popham*, London, 1938, pp.211, 167.

53 Bebbington, *Nonconformist Conscience*, p.90.

54 A. D. Gillies, ed., *Pastor William Wright: some memories and memorials*, Denny, 1927, pp.17, 24.

55 Meyer to James Mursell, 15 Apr.1910, W. Y. Fullerton, *F. B. Meyer: a biography*, London, n.d., p.138.

56 G. B. Marsden, *Fundamentalism and American Culture: the shaping of 20th-century Evangelicalism, 1870-1925*, New York, 1980, pp.91f.

57 Clement Heath to editor, *Baptist Times*, 2 Feb.1950, p.10.

58 W. E. Maddocks to editor, *Baptist Times*, 14 Nov.1935, p.828.

59 H. G. Wood, *T. R. Glover: a biography*, Cambridge, 1953, p.157.

60 T. R. Glover to editor, *Baptist Times*, 3 Nov.1922, p.715.

61 *Baptist Times*, 5 Nov.1931, p.775.

62 *Baptist Times*, 27 Jun.1935, p.475. The episode is analysed in Koss, *Nonconformity in Modern British Politics*, pp.187-215.

63 *Baptist Times*, 21 Dec.1923, p.883.

64 Payne, *Baptist Union*, p.207.

65 C. B. Jewson, *The Baptists in Norfolk*, London, 1957, p.148. Frank Buffard, *Kent and Sussex Baptist Associations*, Faversham, 1963, p.127.

66 Keith Robbins, *The Abolition of War: the 'peace movement' in Britain, 1914-1919*, Cardiff, 1976, p.192.

67 D. A. Martin, *Pacifism: an historical and sociological study*, London, 1965, p.173.

68 John Rae, *Conscience and Politics: the British government and the conscientious objector to military service, 1916-1919*, London, 1970, p.251.

69 T. M. Bassett, *The Welsh Baptists*, Swansea, 1977, pp.388, 391.

70 Morgan, *Rebirth of a Nation*, p.191.

71 Payne, *Baptist Union*, p.207.

72 Martin Ceadel, *Pacifism in Britain, 1914-1945: the defining of a faith*, Oxford, 1980, p.174. W. H. Haden to editor, *Baptist Times*, 13 June 1935, p.440.

73 E.g. Robin Attifield to editor, *Baptist Times*, 10 Mar.1966, p.4.

74 E. A. Payne, *James Henry Rushbrooke, 1870-1947: a Baptist Greatheart*, London, 1954, spec.pp.62f.

75 Geoffrey Shakespeare, 'The Persecution of Baptists in Russia', *The Baptist Quarterly*, 5, 1930, pp.49,51!

76 F. Townley Lord, *Baptist World Fellowship: a short history of the Baptist World Alliance*, London, 1955, p.168.

77 Cf. E. A. Payne, *Thirty Years of the British Council of Churches,
    1942-1972*, London, 1972, pp.29f.

78 Robin Hallett, *Africa since 1875: a modern history*, Ann Arbor, Michi-
    gan, 1974, pp.543-46.

79 Len Addicott, *Cry Angola!*, London, 1962, p.21. I am grateful to Mr
    Addicott for supplementary information about the agitation.

80 G. T. Brake, *Inside the Free Churches*, London, 1964, p.52.

81 Addicott, *Cry Angola!*, pp.92, 105.

82 Ibid., p.104.

83 *Declarations of Conference on Social Questions*,   London, 1959.

84 *The Proceedings of C.O.P.E.C.*,   London, 1924, p.220.

85 W. Vellam Pitts, *Never Old Parchment*, Windsor, 1976, p.89.

86 D. J. Jeremy, John Barfield and K. S. Newman, *A Century of Grace*,
    Southend-on-Sea, 1976, p.32.

87 *Fourth Baptist World Congress*, ed. W. T. Whitley, Toronto, n.d.,
    pp.236-44.

88 B. B. Gilbert, *British Social Policy, 1914-1939*, London, 1970, p.188.
    Middlemas, *Politics in Industrial Society*, p.255.

89 Buffard, *Kent and Sussex Baptist Association*, pp.127, 130.

90 Shakespeare, *Let Candles be brought in*, pp.142-59.

91 *Baptist Times*, 16 May 1929, p.379.

92 Payne, *Baptist Union*, p.201.

93 Ibid., p.244.

94 Henry Townsend, *Robert Wilson Black*, London, 1954, pp.169, 204.

95 Ibid., pp.183 ff.

96 C. W. Black, *The Temperance Problem and the Free Churches*, London,
    1953.

97 Vellam Pitts, *Never Old Parchment*, p.122.

98 *Baptist Times*, 25 Apr.1929, p.303; 16 May 1929, p.375.

99 H. H. Martin to editor, *Baptist Times*, 21 Jun. 1945, p.6; 9 Feb.1850,
    p.4. Morgan, *Rebirth of a Nation*, p.354.

100 *Cambrian News*, 9 Jun.1939, cited by Madgwick, Griffiths and Walker, p.75.

101 Morgan, *Rebirth of a Nation*, pp.354 ff.

102 E. B. Perkins, *Gambling in English Life*, London, 1950, p.22.

103 *Baptist Times*, 1 Oct.1959, p.6; 8 Oct.1959, p.6.

104 Miller, *Electoral Dynamics*, p.227.

105 E. B. Hardy to editor, *Baptist Times*, 7 Apr.1966, p.4.

106 C. A. Oxley to editor, *Baptist Times*, 6 May 1982, p.4.

107 John Capon, *... and there was light: the story of the Nationwide
    Festival of Light*, London, 1972.

108   Roy Wallis and Richard Bland,*Five Years On: report of a survey of participants in the Nationwide Festival of Light Rally in Trafalgar Square, London, on 25 September 1976*, n.p., n.d., p.30.

109   Ibid., p.51.

110   A. D. Gilbert, *The Making of Post-Christian Britain: a history of the secularization of modern society*, London, 1980, pp.148-53.

111   Townsend, *Black*, p.164.

112   Henry Townsend, *The Claims of the Free Churches*, London, 1949, pp.248f.

113   E. A. Payne, 'The Free Churches and the State', *Free Churchmen Unrepentant and Repentant and Other Papers*, London, 1965, pp.56-74.

114   Bebbington, *Nonconformist Conscience*, pp.138f.

115   G. K. A. Bell, *Randall Davidson: Archbishop of Canterbury*, 3rd edn, London, 1952, p.1346. *Baptist Times*, 16 Dec.1910, p.822.

116   James Murphy, *Church, State and Schools in Britain, 1800-1970*, London, 1971, p.108.

117   P. H. J. H. Gosden, *Education in the Second World War: a study in policy and administration*, London, 1976, p.277.

118   Townsend, *Black*, pp.147 ff.

119   *Baptist Times*, 8 Oct.1959, p.17.

120   Christopher Driver, *A Future for the Free Churches?*, London, 1962, p.53.

121   Murphy, *Church, State and Schools*, p.124.

122   *Baptist Times*, 18 Oct. 1951, p.7.

123   J. Ivory Cripps to editor, *Baptist Times*, 24 Nov.1922, p.763.

124   *Seventh Baptist World Congress*, ed. W. O. Lewis, London, 1948, p.66.

125   *Sixth Baptist World Congress*, ed. J. H. Rushbrooke, Atlanta, 1939, pp.203-6. Cf. the essay in this volume by K. W. Clements, 'A Question of Freedom? British Baptists and the German Church Struggle', p.

126   *Report on the Seminar-Consultation of National Baptist Unions of Socialist Countries*, Moscow, 1979, pp.24, 29.

D. W. BEBBINGTON

A QUESTION OF FREEDOM?

BRITISH BAPTISTS AND THE GERMAN CHURCH STRUGGLE

British Baptists and the *German* Church Struggle: the title
sounds somewhat exotic, and the subject may appear to be peripheral to both Baptist life in Britain and German Church history in the 1930s. Was there any significant relation between
the two? Let me just present an imaginary photograph (as far
as I know, no actual photograph exists) of an event which in
itself indicates and symbolises the connexion. It is the
afternoon of 8th August 1934, in an office on the Jebens-
strasse in Berlin. Ludwig Müller, *Reichbischof* of the German
Evangelical Church, stands with a prepared statement in his
hands. He is used to preparing statements, and has done so
repeatedly ever since being appointed plenipotentiary for
Church affairs by Adolf Hitler in the spring of 1933. A
fanatical Nazi, with his previous ecclesiastical experience
being largely in military chaplaincies, he is Hitler's hope
of bringing about a united and tranquil Protestantism loyal
to the Nazi state. In fact Müller's appointment and subsequent
heavy-handed administration has brought only turmoil to the
Evangelical Churches, with mounting opposition to what is seen
as political interference in the spiritual demesne of the
Church. His eventual election as Reichbishop has been hailed by
the so-called *Deutsche Christen* (German Christians, who are
attempting to transmute Christianity into a religion of Aryan
race and mythology) as the proper introduction of the *Führer*
principle, appropriate to a truly German Church in what is -
at last - a truly German *Reich*. So this man, who the previous
September stood by the grave of Martin Luther at Wittenberg to
be acclaimed as Reichbishop amid swastika flags and Nazi
salutes, who personifies the upheaval in the German Church,
stands in his office, greeting his visitors, who include:
J. H. Rushbrooke, M. E. Aubrey, B. Grey Griffith, Gilbert Laws,
F. C. Spurr, C. E. Wilson, S. W. Hughes, James Scott, and C. T.
Le Quesne. Just how and why this meeting took place, and what
was said at it, will be dealt with later.

In fact, when one considers just how much time and interest
is spent by the major denominations in concern for what is
happening in situations of conflict in other parts of the
world, then how British Baptists viewed events in Nazi Germany
is likely to be more than a minor facet of denominational
affairs during the 1930s. Moreover, Nazism being the most
traumatic experience of western Europe this century, and the
response of the Churches to it providing the most searching
test of Christian integrity, it would be exceedingly strange
if an account of Baptist life in this period ignored the issue
altogether. Indeed, this subject provides a classic case-
study in the problems of assessing the rights and wrongs of
behaviour by Christians in contexts which, socially, politically and religiously, are very different from our own.

One thing should be made quite clear at the outset.
Leading Baptist opinion in this country, and popular Baptist
opinion generally, was hostile to Nazism from the outset.
This was no residual Germanophobia left over from 1914-18.
By 1930, the tone of *Baptist Times* articles on international
relations was markedly conciliatory towards Germany, and sym-
pathetic to her desire to be placed on a more equal footing
with France and Italy.   The German sense of injustice at the
Versailles Treaty was acknowledged and, to a degree, supported.
But Hitler and the Nazis were, as early as 1932, recognized
to be "one of the great menaces to the peace of Europe",[1]
and the increasing Nazi vote during 1932-33 was noted with
alarm.   It was the outright militarism, the hostility to any
form of democracy, and above all the violent anti-semitism,
which offended Baptist as other Christian opinion in Britain.
On 30th March 1933 - two months after Hitler's accession to
the chancellorship, one month after the burning of the Reichs-
tag, and three weeks after the final elections in Germany -
the *Baptist Times* commented:

> The accounts of the ill-treatment of Jews in Germany
> came as a shock to the world... The persecution of
> the Jews is a recurrent blot upon the pages of history,
> but Germany has stepped back hundreds of years and
> tarnished a glorious past.   Nothing but evil can come
> of the Hitlerite policy in stirring the passions of
> the people against the Jewish race.   The consequences
> may be and ought to be very severe.   It is no use
> talking of brotherhood while Jews are dragged through
> the streets, their property destroyed, their bodies
> maltreated, even when their lives are spared.   The
> responsible authorities in Germany should put on
> sackcloth and ashes, and lament and seek forgiveness.
> We hope that the entire Christian Church will unite
> in protest against these outrages.[2]

Similarly, two weeks later, the journal condemned the Nazi
boycott of Jewish businesses, stating that the plain lesson
of history was being ignored, that no nation had ever finally
emerged victorious from a struggle with Jewish nationalism.
"It is inextinguishable and the Nazis are not likely to suc-
ceed where far stronger forces than theirs have failed".[3]
Reading these words, as we do now, from the far side of
Auschwitz, we can only admit how tragically they were con-
firmed.   But at least leading Baptists in this country did
quickly perceive the ugly reality of what was going on in
Germany.   They did not have to wait, as did some high-minded
observers, for such bloody episodes as the Röhm massacre of
1934, to be shaken awake.   The Nazi mentality was "overbearing,
intolerant and brutal", extending not only to the persecution
of the Jews but "to all who do not pronounce the Nazi shibbo-
leth".[4]   This needs stating, because of late there has been
a tendency to link nonconformist attitudes to Nazi Germany
mainly with the so-called appeasement policy.   That the peace
movement of the 1930s received powerful nonconformist support
is not in doubt, nor the fact that some of the leading states-
men associated with the Munich policy were of nonconformist

background. But the overwhelming evidence offered by the
Baptist Times is that Nazism was recognized for what it was
from the start by the leaders of Baptist opinion. Nor have
I found evidence of any prominent Baptists who might fit
Stephen Koss's description of Lloyd George's Free Church col-
laborators in his Council of Action. They were, states Koss,
"particularly anxious to achieve an understanding with Germany
in order to ensure peace, and, if possible, to obtain concessions for persecuted Protestants and Jews".[5]

Few features of the new German Reich attracted more attention abroad than the dealings of the authorities with the
churches, both Protestant and Catholic, and with the response
of those churches. In England, a prime source of information
was the London *Times*, among whose informants was G. K. A. Bell,
Bishop of Chichester, and from 1932 Chairman of the Universal
Council for Life and Work. From 1933 onwards, one of his
main sources of first-hand information was Dietrich Bonhoeffer,
who in that year came to London as pastor of the German congregation there. Much comment in the religious press, including the *Baptist Times*, was therefore derivative from that of
the *Times*. Nevertheless, the main contours of the struggle
can be recognized in the columns of the *Baptist Times* from the
early summer of 1933 and the twelve months following, namely:

1. The campaign to unite the various Evangelical (i.e. Protestant) regional (*Land*) churches of Germany into a single
Reich Church; and the campaign by the fanatically nationalist
"German Christians" to introduce a racial basis into the
church, i.e. to exclude non-Aryans from office, corresponding
to the anti-Jewish measures introduced into the German Civil
service and universities.

2. The heavy-handed coercive measures imposed upon the
Evangelical Church, notably the use of state commissars, and,
after his "election" to the position of Reichbishop, the dic-
tatorial administration of Ludwig Müller.

3. The resistance to the coercive methods, the questioning of
the legality of many of the authoritarian methods of Müller,
and the protests by increasing number of pastors at these
measures, and at the dismissal of pastors with Jewish ancestry.

4. The actual dismissal (albeit temporary) of some protesting
pastors (such as Martin Niemöller of Dahlem, Berlin).

5. The Barmen Synod at the end of May 1934, adopting what
became the famous Barmen Confession as the true credal basis
of the German Evangelical Church, with its massive affirmation
of Jesus Christ as the one Word of God to be obeyed in life
and death, and its forthright rejection of the claims of other
powers and beings for lordship over the Church.

Now it is one thing for distant contours to be visible
through the mist, but quite another for the actual shapes and
relationships to each other of the constituent hills and valleys to be discerned. The issues and course of events in the
Church Struggle were confused for many even within Germany,
let alone for those viewing it from without, and with very

incomplete understanding of the context. Keith Robbins points
out that there was widespread ignorance in Britain of the
nature of German church life, the structure of the Protestant
Churches and different elements within them. This vagueness
was to manifest itself even in the terminology used: "Was it,
for example, the Confessing Church or the Confessional Church?"[6]
Even more fundamentally, one suspects that relatively few
readers of the *Baptist Times* would have perceived that "Evangelical" in the German context simply means "Protestant" and
does not carry the particular connotations of "evangelicalism"
as it does in England. Consider, for instance, the following
note in the *Baptist Times* "Table Talk" of 11th January 1934:

> On Monday the struggle between the parties in the
> German Protestant Church began in dead earnest.
> Nine meetings, which took the form of public worship,
> were called by the Evangelical party. Three were
> forbidden by Dr Müller, the Reich Primate, or the
> police. The Cathedral was closed, but other meetings
> were arranged and were held before there was time for
> for them to be banned. The Evangelical party protests
> against the policy of identifying religion and nation-
> alism, and complains that Christians have not now the
> right to meet in the land of Luther.

In fact *all* "parties" in the Church struggle considered themselves "Evangelical". But many British observers must have
concluded from accounts like the above, that those who were
opposing Müller and the "German Christians" were the especially
devout and scripturally orthodox. There were two main consequences of this confused apperception of German churchmanship.

First, there was a vastly over-simplified version of precisely who the main contestants in the struggle were. On
14th December 1933 the *Baptist Times* reported:

> Protestantism has won the first round in the conflict
> with Hitlerism which threatened to destroy it as a
> Christian Church. All other parties in the Reich,
> racial, social, and political, have been destroyed;
> Protestantism alone has successfully resisted Hitler's
> dictatorship and survived in the struggle. Hitler's
> instrument in this attempt to make the Church a part
> of the Nazi state was the sect known as the "German
> Christians". The name is a misnomer, for they are
> Nazis first and Christians only in name. If these
> "German Christians" had their way, Jews and other
> non-Aryans would be excluded from membership of the
> Church; the Old Testament would be rejected as "a
> collection of Jewish legends"; the swastika would
> rank with the Cross, and Jesus would only be one
> figure in a Nordic pantheon alongside of Thor and
> Odin.

The picture given of "German Christian" aims and beliefs is
accurate, but not so the estimation of the place of the movement in official Nazi policy towards the churches. The model
with which the writer works is that of, first, Hitler's own
attempts to bring about a Nazified Church in a Nazi state,

and second, his use of the German Christians as a kind of
religious storm troop brigade towards this end. In fact,
Hitler remained studiously evasive and ambiguous as to his
aims for the churches. Privately contemptuous of Christianity
in both its Catholic and Protestant forms, and cherishing as
a long-term aim the withering away of support for organized
religion, he nevertheless recognized the political necessity
of containing the churches as long as they were in existence,
and seeking their political support for the Nazi State.
His famous, or infamous, speech of 23rd March 1933 spoke of
his support for "positive Christianity" in the new Germany,
and for the historic traditions of both Catholicism and Protestantism as the spiritual basis of Germany now as before.[7]
Hitler's hope was that Müller would bring peace to the factions
in the Protestant camp, and Müller's increasing failure to do
this cost him the favour of the Nazi hierarchy. The German
Christians, likewise, while loudly claiming to be Hitler's
spiritual wing, were regarded with some suspicion by Hitler,
who suspected that most of the German Christians were simply
time-serving opportunists out for preferment.[8] Above all,
a passage such as that just quoted assumes that outside the
ranks of the German Christians, Protestantism was a single,
homogeneous whole, loyal to the pure faith of the Reformation,
and unequivocal in its opposition to interference by the Nazi
State. None of us should need reminding that there is no such
thing as the pure Reformation faith: or rather, there is the
Reformation of Luther, and that of Calvin, and of Zwingli, and
so on. The German Evangelical Church consisted of Lutheran
Churches, Reformed Churches, and United Churches. Nor were
these titles merely decorative, even in the twentieth century.
As the Church Struggle wore on, even within the Confessing
Church, divisions appeared, some along these traditional
theological lines. The more quiescent Lutheran stance towards
the State, and - particularly under the rejuvenating influence
of Karl Barth - the more activist Reformed attitude, emerged
again. Much of the Church Struggle was a struggle within the
Churches, as well as against the State.

    Much of this highly important detail was inaccessible to
the British observers. But there was a notable exception as
far as Baptists were concerned. In November 1933 the *Baptist
Times* carried an article "The German Church and the Christian
Jew", on the debate within the church on the Aryan clauses,
and giving a full account of the findings of the Marburg University theologians' acceptance of orders of race and culture
in the church.[9] The author was R. Birch Hoyle, a Baptist
minister who was probably the leading Baptist authority on
continental theology at that time, being the translator of
several German works, including two by Karl Barth, and the
author of a book on Barth's theology. For Baptist understanding of the Church Struggle, it was unfortunate that during
the crucial two years 1934-36 he was in America as Professor
at Mid-Western Theological Seminary. He died in 1939. In
the article just mentioned, however, even Hoyle refers to
Hitler's policy of "excluding non-Aryans from office within
the Churches".

The second main consequence of the confusion, and one
directly brought about by the first, was a repeated and ex-
aggerated optimism regarding the outcome of the struggle.
Time and again the *Baptist Times* reported a "victory" for the
Evangelicals, or the "Confessionals", or even for "Protestantism". It was made to seem as though the whole church had
staunchly resisted the Nazi State, when in fact a section of
that church, the Confessing Church, had refused to compromise
either with the "German Christians", or, later, with the more
moderate of the Lutherans. This in turn meant that interest
tended to be lost after each minor "victory", until the next
wave of arrests or other repressive measures, and the denominational press more than amply illustrates the comment of
Eberhard Bethge in his biography of Dietrich Bonhoeffer: "The
concern of the western ecumenicals was to a large extent determined by practical - that is to say, political - considerations;
consequently, when the struggle became a tedious contest for
the Confession, their interest flagged, to flare up again as
soon as there was any sensational news of police action in
Germany".[10]

This remark of Bethge points to another factor in the way
foreign observers perceived the struggle. The difficulties
we have so far considered are those inevitably attached to
viewing a situation from a distance. But, in addition, what
we see in any controversy will partly be determined by what
we expect to see, or even wish to see. We bring our presuppositions with us. Baptists, in particular, had their own
presuppositions regarding a conflict involving both Church
and State. If it does not sound too provocative, Baptists
like others viewed the world through ideological spectacles,
and the ideology in their case was that of religious freedom.
It may be thought impertinent to describe such a cherished
tenet of Baptists as an ideology. By an ideology is meant
here a fundamental idea on the ordering of human society,
usually with a philosophical, metaphysical or theological
basis, and serving the interests of a particular group in
that society. The characteristic Baptist belief in freedom
of belief, worship and witness for all people in society
matches this definition. This is not to say whether it is
right or wrong. But because it is a conceptual framework as
to what is paramount and necessary, we do have to bear in
mind the way in which it can, if allowed sole rights, distort
as well as illuminate our judgment of reality, our assessment
of the issues in any situation. This took place with the
assessment by British Baptists of the Church situation in
Germany during the Third Reich.

On 1st June 1933, the *Baptist Times* carried two paragraphs
stating that the Nazis were aiming to unite all the Protestant
churches, including the Baptists, into a single German Evangelical Church. "Probably even the Nazis, in their passion
for centralisation and uniformity, would not try to convert
Baptists into Paedobaptists by force. Some latitude in faith
and practice would have to be allowed, even in a Nazi State
Church, but the German Baptists are gravely disturbed at the
prospect of being compelled to surrender their independence

and become members of a State Church predominantly Lutheran".
Thus at once, attention was focussed on the instinctive, traditional fear of Baptists everywhere. It was the case, moreover, that as far as the German Baptists were concerned, this
was the *only* anxiety they had about the Nazi State. During
the summer of 1933 the German Baptist journal, *Wahrheitszeuge*,
complained bitterly about the *Baptist Times*'s criticisms of
the new Germany. In contrast to British Baptist misgivings
about Hitler, their German counterparts claimed:

> The decisive fact is beyond question the revolt
> against the perils of Bolshevism and the will to
> lead the German people by thorough-going renewal
> to a new level of moral and national strength.
> The thought of leadership, of course, outweighs
> dogmatic democracy and thus creates a new type of
> State.[11]

The German government was strongly inclined towards peace,
claimed the *Wahrheitszeuge*, and the English brethren could
serve their own and the German interests best by clearly recognising "the deep and genuine national and moral powers
underlying the German temper, and in the light of this recognition judge the matters which are non-essentials". The controversy between the *Wahrheitszeuge* and J. C. Carlile, editor
of the *Baptist Times*, continued throughout the summer. The
German Baptists, led by Paul Schmidt,[12] complained of British
lack of understanding of the "real" aims and spirit of Nazism,
and by "non-essentials" evidently meant the outbreaks of persecution against the Jews. On the German Baptist side, there
was continual evasion of the anti-semitic issue. J. H. Rushbrooke, General Secretary of the Baptist World Alliance, who
probably had a personal knowledge of Germany unsurpassed by
any English churchman of the period, returned from a visit to
the German Baptist Union Assembly in September 1933 and reported that "the overwhelming majority of German Baptists
welcome the Nazi Government with the Chancellorship of Herr
Hitler, chiefly on the ground that it has averted the peril
of atheist-Communist domination".

Rushbrooke had particular reason for concern with Germany
just then, quite apart from the political situation and its
possible implications for German Baptists. The Fourth Congress
of the Baptist World Alliance had taken place in 1928 in
Toronto. The Fifth Congress had been planned to take place
in Berlin in the summer of 1933, but late in 1932 the Executive
of the Alliance decided to postpone the event due to the fin-
ancial crisis.[13] In November 1933 the venue for the Congress,
now planned for August 1934, was still unsettled when the
Alliance Executive met again in New York. An invitation had
been received from Switzerland, but the German Baptists had
also renewed their former invitation. The German Baptists had,
prior to inviting the Alliance, sought and received assurance
from the new German government that the Congress would be welcome, and the Minister of Information himself, Dr Goebbels,
had even sent a telegram to the Alliance expressing his cordial
sympathy and hope that the invitation would be accepted.[14] If

in retrospect such a communication has a sinister flavour, at
the time the issues seemed less clear-cut. In the event, the
Executive decided upon Berlin. The strong misgivings felt in
some countries about political conditions in Germany were
taken into account but the overriding considerations were "the
claims of Christian fraternity". Dr F. W. Simoleit, Director
of the German Baptist Missionary Society and Vice-President of
the BWA, had assured the Executive that German Baptists were
wholeheartedly desirous of the Congress coming, and they had
refrained from issuing the invitation until assured by the
Nazi government that the Congress would be welcome - and
indeed, after showing Reich ministers an outline of the programme which would include sessions on such matters as race,
nationalism and peace.[15]   Rushbrooke stated that in view of
all this, it was impossible to refuse the invitation:

> It would have the appearance of a definite slight to
> the German Baptists. It was also felt to be unfitting
> that differing opinions concerning the policy of
> governments should be allowed to check our expression
> of Christian unity through the Congress, or to inter-
> rupt a fraternal co-operation which has been main-
> tained through many years. At precisely such a time
> as this, the hand of friendship should be firmly
> grasped.[16]

Rushbrooke passionately and sincerely believed in the necessity of a World Congress, not only in creating and fostering
relationships among Baptists, but as a demonstration by Baptists that the freedom and spontaneity of "fraternity" was as
effective a means of unity as hierarchical authority. "The
present age fiercely challenges our ideas of liberty and self-
government. Organisation tends more and more to extinguish
freedom. Liberty can be vindicated only by demonstrating
that it works".[17]   Of course, stated Rushbrooke, it had to be
asked whether Baptists in Berlin would be able "freely to express their religious and ethical convictions without grave
risk of conflict with the political authorities, through
which the Baptists of Germany might suffer".[18]   Indeed,
suspicion might have fallen on the German Baptists had their
invitation been refused.

Not all were convinced by these arguments. Many Americans
were deeply worried about the wider implications of the Baptist world family meeting in the Nazi capital. M. E. Aubrey,
General Secretary of the Baptist Union, was taken aback by
the strength of American feeling when in New York in the early
summer of 1934, and had misgivings about attending Berlin right
up to the last moment. J. C. Carlile had even stronger doubts,
and expressed them in a *Baptist Times* leader under his own
name almost on the eve of the Congress.

> Baptists by conviction and tradition are opposed to
> the State control of religion. They stand for liberty
> and for the sacredness of personality. Their witness
> is worldwide and cannot be silenced in any nation,
> even though some adherents of the Baptist communion
> may waver in their allegiance and be attracted by the

glamour of the religion of Nationalism. Berlin may
be the acid test of modern Baptists. The dilemma is
serious. Silence on the part of the leaders concerning
recent developments which have been a definite interference with religious liberty may be interpreted in
many countries as acceptance on the part of Baptists,
or at least acquiescence in the new order and concerning recent happenings. Such silence would be
regarded as a betrayal of principle and lack of
fidelity to those truths for which our sires did not
hesitate to sacrifice their lives.[19]

Arguments both for going and not going to Berlin were therefore conducted in terms of the ideology of religious liberty.
Either way, the Congress took place as planned, in August 1934.
In many ways it was an impressive event. 8,000 attended,
including nearly 300 from Great Britain. It was the largest
international gathering to have met in Berlin since the Great
War, and, with the exception of the Olympic Games in 1936,
may have been the largest in the Nazi period altogether.
Freedom there certainly was in the public sessions. An
address of welcome by the Burgomeister of Berlin extolling
the virtues of the new Germany was followed by Rushbrooke
courteously but firmly pointing out that there were many in
the audience who would not agree with all that had been said.
The Congress suspended one of its sessions in order to listen
to the broadcast of the funeral of President Hindenburg - an
event which certainly gave participants a sense of sharing in
another dramatic moment in Germany's destiny.

The previous Congress had set up five commissions on topics
which included nationalism and racialism. These now reported
to the Congress, there was public discussion, and the passing
of resolutions. The report on nationalism was given by N. J.
Nordström of Sweden in a balanced document which set out the
case for a qualified love of country, subject to the supreme
lordship of Christ in all ethical matters. "Nationalistic
sentiments involve a danger to the Christian Church, because
they weaken the sense of responsibility for a universal
Christian service and limit the Christian outlook".[20]   In response, Paul Schmidt, editor of *Wahrheitszeuge*, stated the
belief in nationality as an order of creation, and in the
sharp distinction between the two realms of the Church, where
the law of love operates, and the world of the peoples, where
the iron law of force and conflict holds good. "The spirit
of the nations is a healthy nationalism. Facts of blood,
speech, and mental outlook are a natural innate gift to a
people...".[21]   C. E. Wilson, Secretary of the BMS, introduced
the report on Racialism, which included a denunciation of
anti-Semitism, especially on the part of professedly Christian
nations. The public resolutions passed on these and related
topics were equally clear in their enunciation of principles.
That on "Church and State" reaffirmed the freedom of the Church
from State interference. That on racialism condemned "all
racial animosity, and every form of oppression or unfair dis-
crimination toward the Jews, toward coloured people, or toward
subject races in any part of the world".[22]   That on war and

peace called all Christians to witness against the "inhumanity
and anti-Christian character of war" and to promote the cause
of peace. Certainly there was an atmosphere of freedom inside
the Congress hall. M. E. Aubrey made full use of it in addressing the youth rally, on "Young Baptists and Their Tradition":

> We stand for liberty of conscience in all matters
> of faith, liberty to speak and worship as the Spirit
> of God directs us, and we stand for a free, un-
> fettered Church. A Church that is not free to go
> as God directs it cannot carry out its task of
> saving humanity. To bind the Church is to tie the
> hands of God. We stand by the noble declaration of
> the Synod of Barmen which ended on June 1.[23]

Aubrey left unsaid precisely who "we" represented here. Did
it, for instance, include the German Baptists? It seemed hard
to reconcile allegiance to such principles as Aubrey stated,
with the eulogy of Hitler delivered by Carl Schneider of the
Hamburg Baptist Seminary, commemorating the centenary of the
birth of the German Baptist movement, the baptism of J. G.
Oncken in 1834:

> The Centenary of the German Baptists synchronises with
> the re-birth of the German nation as a people. God
> the Lord has given us, in Adolf Hitler, a man who
> recognises the needs of the time and its perils, and
> who is directing and using the forces that make for
> health in order to subdue those that make for decay.
> As a force making for health, the German Baptist
> community has been recognised and used by the Third
> Reich and actively included in the process of renewal.
> Never before has our movement experienced so much in
> the way of public recognition and support as in the
> Third Reich, and to-day in Berlin.[24]

That "increase in public recognition and support" seemed to
be evidenced in the widespread press coverage of the congress
in Germany - except for the fact that details of the resolutions on race and international relations were omitted from
the newspapers; not to mention the fact that the *Baptist Times*
was not allowed to be sold at the Congress. But, for leaders
of the BWA, including those from Britain, the high-point of
the Congress was the meeting which was arranged with Reichbishop Müller. The statement he read was an assurance that
there was no intention whatsoever of incorporating the Baptists of Germany into a State Church. Rushbrooke expressed
the gratitude of all Baptists for this assurance, and courteously stated that it would be deeply hurtful to Baptists
everywhere if those in the *Reich* were coerced in matters
sacred to the conscience. One of the party, on leaving the
Reichbishop's office, told Rushbrooke that it had been worth
coming to Berlin simply to hear this assurance.

Afterwards Rushbrooke was forever insistent on the right-
ness of the Congress going to Berlin. He listed four reasons.
It had convinced the German Baptists of the reality of fraternal fellowship through the BWA. Second, it had secured a

better understanding of the "loyalty to principle which
characterises the German Baptists". German Baptists had not
wavered in their witness to spiritual freedom and the duty of
the church of Christ to serve men of whatever race and nationality. Third, it had strengthened the probability that the
German Baptists would be permitted to continue their work as
a free community. The freely given assurance of Bishop Müller
was of cardinal importance here. Finally, the Baptist world
communion had demonstrated its solidarity on great moral issues. "The world knows where Baptists stand on nationalism
and racialism, international peace and the relations of Church
and State, and our positions were no less definitely stated
than they would have been in London or New York or Paris".[25]
But equally. others such as Aubrey were still not entirely
happy. A careful reading of the Congress Report reveals sufficient inconsistency to add fuel to whatever suspicions
there may have been. It was not just the lack of *full* press
coverage of important issues, though this was clear enough
demonstration that freedom of speech is worthless without the
freedom to be *heard*. It was rather the fact that nowhere in
public discussion did concern move from the general to the
particular, from the abstract to the concrete. Rushbrooke
could say that the world knew where Baptists stood on issues
such as racialism - and indeed gratitude was expressed to the
BWA for the resolutions passed on anti-semitism by the *Jewish
Chronicle*. Unfortunately, any real cutting edge that the
Report of the Commission on Racialism and the Resolution might
have had was removed when C. E. Wilson, in presenting the
Report to the Congress, stated: "It is not to be interpreted
as an attack upon any particular persons, parties, or governments".[26] Was this really an exercise of freedom, freedom for
the ministry of prophecy? Most disconcerting of all, from
the British Baptist point of view, was the disclosure after
the Congress that the banning of the sale of the *Baptist Times*
in Berlin was directed not by the police but by the German
Baptist Union. What price fraternity, let alone freedom, now?

All this jars on ears attuned to glorifying accounts of the
growth of the Baptist movement throughout the world, and puts
some serious questions to the values implicit in world denominational and confessional groupings. In fact, the horrible
suspicion remains that, while Berlin 1934 was an inspiring
occasion for those present, it was also a propaganda device
by the Nazi authorities. Only days after the Congress, the
Lutheran Bishop of Bavaria, Meiser, objected to the use of
force to settle church disputes, police harrassment of pastors,
the banning of meetings, etc. The reply from the authorities
pointed to the fact that the Baptist World Congress had been
assured of freedom of faith by the Reich leadership, and that
the Congress had accepted that assurance.[27]   No wonder Dr
Goebbels had been eager for the Baptists to come to Berlin.
In itself, the ideology of religious liberty proved too naive,
for both the brutal power and the subtleties of the totalitarian state, which could manipulate that ideology for its
own ends. The regime could safely grant a measure of such
liberty to a Baptist community which, because of its small

size and other-worldly outlook, posed no threat to the state's
existence.

The Baptist emphasis on liberty, from 1934 onwards, clouded
the issues of Christian responsibility in Nazi Germany, for,
in the eyes of some, a maintenance of some semblance of liberty and independence more than justified large-scale acquiescence
in the Nazi state. Rushbrooke was irritated by a remark in the
Baptist Times in October 1934: "Up to the present the smaller
communities have seemed to adopt the slogan 'Safety First'.
The honour beongs to those Evangelicals who have stood up and
declared their opposition to the laws which destroy private
judgment and the essential features of the Gospel".[28] Rushbrooke
retorted that the full support of the German Baptists for the
BWA ,Congress resolution on Church and State itself refuted
this idea.[29]   They had not lowered the Baptist flag. He continued, significantly:

> If it should be said that many German Baptists are
> National Socialists, the reply is, of course, that
> they emphasise certain aspects of National Socialism
> which have not received emphasis here. They are
> certainly not anti-Semitic. The Confessional Church,
> so far as public utterances of its leaders go, is as
> emphatically pro-Nazi as any group in the Reich.[30]

Rushbrooke's remark about the pro-Nazi political stance of
the Confessing Church leaders should be noted as a fairly
accurate, if surprising, judgment. A few days later, Rushbrooke went on record as saying that those who wished the
German Free Churches to "make the welkin ring" with protests
against anti-semitism etc. should reflect on the smallness
of their numbers - the Baptists alone amounting to less than
one in a thousand of the population.

Rushbrooke's plea for sympathy with German Baptists notwithstanding, in the succeeding years Baptist instincts in
this country were emphatically with the Confessing Church,
and specifically, from the time of his arrest in 1937, with
Martin Niemöller, the symbol of Christian defiance to the
regime. But again - as Keith Robbins has demonstrated - the
grounds of support for Niemöller and the Confessing Church
in this country was the ideology of religious freedom. While
indeed there was recognition that the Confessing Church was
standing "for the gospel", it was basically seen as a fight
for "freedom". Indeed, the most substantial account of the
Church Struggle to appear before the war, by A. S. Duncan-
Jones, Dean of Chichester, was called *The Struggle for Religious Freedom in Germany*.[31]   The title does not do justice to
the contents, which record in considerable detail the *confessional* element in the Protestant resistance. At the Berlin
Congress Aubrey had lauded the Barmen statement as a charter
of religious freedom. Yet there is nothing in the Barmen
Confession about such freedom. It is about obedience to Jesus
Christ as the one Word of God for the Church.[32]   The main inspiration behind the Barmen Confession was of course Karl
Barth, who maintained his own integrity in refusing to take
the oath of loyalty to Hitler enjoined on university teachers,
and had therefore to return to his native Switzerland.

Barth visited Britain in 1937, and spoke to gatherings of
churchmen in London and in Scotland. Rushbrooke acted as
interpreter at the London meeting. Barth was somewhat disturbed to find so much concern with the "liberty" issue in
this country. Asked what the British churches could do to
aid the Confessing Church, his answer was somewhat surprising.
Two articles from him appeared in the *British Weekly* in 1937
on the subject. Dismissing the idea of protest resolutions
as completely futile and counter-productive as far as their
effect on the Nazi regime was concerned, Barth went on:

> The fact that "freedom of conscience" and "freedom of
> the Church" are approved in Britain and that all
> atrocities are detested and that these views find
> ready expression is well known in Germany; but it
> makes not the slightest impression on the National
> Socialists, or they do not comprehend it. And the
> Confessional Church is not thereby helped, because
> the fight is not about the freedom, but about the
> necessary bondage, of the conscience; and not about
> the freedom, but about the substance, of the Church,
> i.e. about the preservation, rediscovery and authen-
> tication of the true Christian faith. It is not
> waiting to hear the voice of the British citizen
> saying once again what every stout Briton has been
> saying for many centuries, but the voice of the
> British Christian, the voice of the Church in
> Britain, saying now that which can only be said in
> the Holy Spirit, only in recollection of what the
> Holy Scriptures say.[33]

The core of the struggle, Barth states, is about the *content*
of the Christian confession, the response to the Nazi claim
that alongside the revelation of God in Jesus Christ there is
a revelation in nature, history etc. This was the matter of
the Barmen statement.

> Dear brothers and friends in the Church of Great Britain
> and of all other countries, the only real help, apart
> from your prayers, which you can render the German
> Church, would consist in this: in your declaring with
> as much publicity and solemnity as was done in Barmen
> itself that in your conviction also, a conviction
> arising from Holy Scripture, this statement with its
> positive and negative content is the right and
> necessary expression of the Christian faith for our
> day and therefore also your confession of faith.

Barth referred to the way in which the reforming Churches of
the sixteenth century helped each other by reciprocally recognising their confessions.

> The Churches abroad would have to help the German
> Confessional Church by making it known that they
> are one with it - not in disapprobation of Hitler
> and his methods and aims, not in the idea of freedom
> of conscience or of the Church, but in the theological
> presuppositions of the conflict it is waging...

In the light of Barth's trenchant opposition to protests and
demonstrations, one can the more easily see why, as Keith
Robbins has shown,[34] such a figure as Aubrey felt deeply
hesitant over signing a letter to be sent to the German government in protest over Nazi oppression. But what is equally
apparent is that Barth's call for solidarity with the Barmen
Confession fell on completely deaf ears in Britain, on Baptist
ears no less than others. Indeed, any serious discussion of
the *theology* of the German situation is conspicuously meagre
in Baptist writing of the period.[35] British Baptists persisted
in arguing over the issues in terms of religious liberty, thus
preventing any real challenge being offered to the German
Baptists - who were always able to reply that they *had* more
than enough liberty to worship and witness - and shielding
themselves from the real theological challenge of the German
crisis and the Barmen Confession. Even the Baptist Union
Assembly resolution of 1938 subsumed the question of persecution of the Jews under the matter of *religious* liberty.

So the struggle wore on, with British Baptists continually
identifying with the Confessing Church opposition, and German
Baptist apologists maintaining that full religious liberty was
theirs under Hitler, and that as a result they were prospering
(their numbers increased in 1935). Confessing Church leaders,
the German Baptists maintained, were simply suffering the consequences of breaking laws to which, as members of a State
Church, they were in duty bound to submit. Indeed, this aspect
of the struggle was curiously overlooked by many British Baptists, who seemed to think that the German Church crisis was
primarily a vindication of the principle of *separation* of
Church from State. In 1937 the whole issue of comparisons
between the Confessing Church and the German Free Churches
boiled over as a result of the behaviour of the two German
Free Church delegates at the Oxford "Life and Work" Conference
on Church, Community and State. Bishop Otto Melle of the German Methodists, and Paul Schmidt, Secretary of the German Baptists, were the only two German delegates. The Evangelical
Church invitations had been sent to the Confessing Church,
but they had been refused permission to travel by the government. It was the unanimous decision of the conference to send
a message of fraternal greeting and sympathy to the Evangelical
opposition - unanimous, that is, but for the last-minute opposition by Melle and Schmidt, who stated that under Hitler they
had no grounds for complaint and much for rejoicing. Free
Churchmen, particularly, were incensed by this apparent betrayal, and the issue spilled into the pages of the *Baptist
Times*.[36]

In this correspondence, it was E. A. Payne who took the
initiative, with a plea for understanding of the German Baptist stance, pointing out that "the German Baptist movement
is little more than one hundred years old, and that until the
seventies of last century it was persecuted by both the
Established Church and the State. Even to recent times the
ecclesiastical authorities have been cool, if not contemptuous,
in their attitude towards the Free Churches of Germany".[37]

Payne pointed out that from whatever motives, the Nazi regime
had secured more religious freedom for the Baptists, and the
dispute within the Evangelical Church did not seem to concern
them. Then, provocatively, he asked: "Before condemning our
brethren, let us ask ourselves what would have been the attitude of an English Baptist in the 18th or early 19th century,
if he had witnessed a quarrel between the Anglican Church and
the State, even if it had resulted in the imprisonment of a
few Bishops". This touched other Baptist nerves on the raw,
prompting vigorous replies from P. T. Thomson, H. N. Philcox,
and E. Amos.[38]   The correspondents felt that Payne had slighted
the concern of Baptist forebears for freedom *for all*. Payne
defended himself by saying, first, that he agreed with the
correspondents' siding with the Confessing Church (but pointed
out that the struggle was being conducted in a world of
thought very different from the British); and secondly, by
stating: "I think our forefathers of those days would have
been saddened by any persecution of men for conscience' sake,
but they would have regarded such a struggle as in large
measure the consequences of the State establishment of religion, and had the State at the same time secured for them
greater freedom I am not at all sure that they would immediately have intervened in the conflict".[39]   Even more pertin-
ently, Payne pointed out that in this country it was but a
few years since certain Free Churchmen had themselves joined
in a campaign to prevent the Established Church from revising
its Prayer Book in accordance with its own wishes.

For his part, Aubrey was deeply unsettled by what had
happened at Oxford – inspired by the ecumenical experience
(his first on the large scale), but depressed by the stance
of his German counterparts. "There were no words of sympathy
for their suffering brothers of the Evangelical and Roman
Catholic Churches, nor of condemnation of the treatment of
the Jews, who include many Jewish Christians".[40]   He saw, too,
that their much vaunted "religious freedom" was due in large
measure to their almost negligible place in Germany. "It is
convenient window-dressing". Moreover, stated Aubrey frankly,
now that the German Free Churchmen had openly praised Hitler
before their Christian brethren, they could no longer claim
to be non-political. Their consciences must be left to themselves and to God. "They, on their part, must realise that
their fellow-believers in Britain and America cannot stand by
them, for we have our tradition of protest against every form
of tyranny".

T. G. Dunning, of the Baptist Union Young People's Department and Chairman of the BWA Youth Committee, however, was
not so sure that the German Baptists should be written off.
Both the Moral and Social Questions Committee of the BU and
the Executive of the BWA declined to protest to the German BU
over their attitudes.

> Moreover, assuming that the German Baptist Union are
> altogether wrong, ought we not, as members of one
> great Baptist family, to discuss these things in
> public, but with one another alone? This seems more

in accord with Matthew 18, and is certainly the
procedure   adopted at the above-mentioned Committee
meeting.[41]

Whether such frank and private talks with the German Baptists ever were pursued is not known to the writer. In the
official BWA Report of the Commission studying the findings
of the 1937 Oxford and Edinburgh conferences, we read that
the Oxford message to the Christian Churches "met with general
approval, although with some exceptions. German brethren,
and to less extent other Continental Europeans, deplored what
they regarded as political deliverances. These felt that such
conferences should not become involved in what are properly
political functions".[42]

When the BWA Congress met in Atlanta in August 1939,
Aubrey's address "Christianity and the Totalitarian State",
with its forthright denunciation of Nazism, and its declaration of support for Niemöller and the persecuted Evangelicals,
was followed by Paul Schmidt's address on "Liberalism, Collectivism and the Baptists".[43] Schmidt, predictably, acted as
apologist for the state of affairs in Germany *and* claimed
political neutrality. On the basis of the gospel there is
nothing to choose between liberalism and collectivism. "We
do not believe that Christian and Baptist ideals are necessarily identical with any political ideology".[44] The question
of whether certain political ideologies are *incompatible* with
Christianity, however, was studiously avoided.

By now, of course, the war was almost upon the world.
Only after the defeat of Nazi Germany could British Baptists
begin a dialogue with a new generation of their brethren in
Germany. Only then did it really dawn on Baptists in Germany,
and to some extent in Britain as well, that the ideal of
religious freedom by itself is insufficient as a criterion of
the justice of a government, and the public witness of the
church. There are other items on the agenda of prophecy.
Only a few weeks before the Atlanta Congress, a member of the
German Confessing Church on a short visit to America, wrote
these words in New York:

> America calls herself the land of the free. Under
> this term today she understands the right of the
> individual to independent thought, speech and action.
> In this context, religious freedom is, for the
> American, an obvious possession... Thus freedom
> here means possibility, the possibility of unhindered
> activity given by the world to the church.
>
> Now if the freedom of the church is essentially
> understood as this possibility, then the concept is
> still unrecognised. The freedom of the church is
> not where it has possibilities, but only where the
> Gospel really and in its own power makes room for
> itself on earth, even and precisely when no such
> possibilities are offered to it. The essential
> freedom of the Church is not a gift of the world
> to the church, but the freedom of the Word of God

itself to gain a hearing... Whether the churches
or God are really free can only be decided by the
actual preaching of the Word of God. Only where
this word can be preached concretely, in the midst
of historical reality, in judgment, command, forgiveness of sinners and liberation from all human
institutions is there freedom of the church.
But where thanks for institutional freedom must be
rendered by the sacrifice of freedom of preaching,
the church is in chains, even if it believes itself
to be free.[45]

That is a message which both British and German Baptists
would have benefited from hearing, at Atlanta in 1939 if not
in Berlin in 1934. But as the delegates were sailing east-
wards across the Atlantic in that last summer of peace,
Dietrich Bonhoeffer was sailing westwards, back to the Germany
where he was to live and die as a demonstration of what
Christian freedom is, in the end, actually all about.

NOTES

1 *Baptist Times* (BT), 10th March 1933.

2 BT, 30th March 1933.

3 BT, 13th April 1933.

4 BT, 22nd June 1933.

5 S. Koss, *Nonconformity in Modern British Politics*, London 1975. p.190 f.

6 K. Robbins, "Martin Niemöller, the German Church Struggle, and English
   Opinion", *Journal of Ecclesiastical History*, Vol.XXI, No.2, (April
   1970), p.149.

7 For this statement and much other documentation on Nazism and the
   churches, see P. Matheson, *The Third Reich and the Christian Churches*,
   Edinburgh, 1981.

8 A useful overall assessment of Nazi policy towards the churches, and
   the various groupings in the struggle is J. S. Conway, *The Nazi Persecution of the Churches 1933-1945*, London 1968.

9 BT, 16th November 1933.

10 E. Bethge, *Dietrich Bonhoeffer*, London 1970, p.298.

11 BT, 18th May 1933.

12 General Secretary of the German Baptist Union and editor of the
   Wahrheitszeuge.

13 BWA reports make clear that it was the international economic outlook
   at least as much as the uncertainty of the German situation which led
   to postponement of the Congress.

14 BT, 2nd November 1933.

15 BT, 30th November 1933.

16 Ibid.

17   BT, 11th January 1934.

18   BT, 5th May 1934.

19   BT, 2nd August 1934.

20   *Fifth Baptist World Congress, Official Report*, ed. J. H. Rushbrooke, London, 1934, p.34.

21   ibid., p.64.

22   ibid., p.17.

23   ibid., p.182.

24   ibid., p.192 f.

25   ibid., p.v f.

26   ibid., p.64.

27   BT, 6th September 1934.

28   BT, 18th October 1934.

29   BT, 25th October 1934.

30   ibid.

31   London, 1938.

32   Matheson, op.cit., pp.45-47. A full version of the Barmen Confession may be found in E. H. Robertson, *Christians Against Hitler*, London 1962, pp.48-52.

33   *British Weekly*, 22nd April 1937.

34   K. Robbins, "Free Churchmen and the Twenty Years' Crisis", *Baptist Quarterly*, Vol. XXVII, No. 8 (October 1978), esp. p.353 f.

35   In addition to the work of R. Birch Hoyle cited earlier, an exception is G. J. M. Pearce, "The State as God", *Baptist Quarterly*, Vol. IX, No. 7 (July 1939), pp.409-416.

36   Birch Hoyle, who was also present at Oxford, was evidently so embarrassed by the behaviour of Melle and Schmidt, that in his report of the conference for the *British Weekly*, 22nd July 1937, he made no mention of the episode.

37   BT, 29th July 1937.

38   BT, 5th August 1937.

39   BT, 12th August 1937.

40   BT, 29th July 1937.

41   BT, 26th August, 1937.

42   *Sixth Baptist World Congress, Official Report*, ed. J. H. Rushbrooke, Atlanta, 1939, p.130.

43   ibid., pp.198-206.

44   ibid., p.203.

45   Dietrich Bonhoeffer, "Protestantism without Reformation", in *No Rusty Swords*, ed. E. H. Robertson, London 1965, p.104 f.

K. W. CLEMENTS

TOWARDS AN APPRECIATION OF BAPTIST ARCHITECTURE

> My notions of architecture are not worth much, because
> I look at a building from a theological point of view,
> not from an architectural one. It seems to me that
> there are two sacred languages in the world. There
> was the Hebrew of old, and ... Greek ... Our fullest
> revelation of God's will is in that tongue ... The
> standard of our faith is Greek ... Greek is the sacred
> tongue, and Greek is the Baptist's tongue ... and this
> shall be a Grecian place of worship...[1]

Thus Charles Haddon Spurgeon, a naughty proof that a theology
of architecture supposedly based on the Bible may be as unhelp-
ful a guide to church building as any other. Spurgeon apart,
this paper has two points of departure, together with one
purpose and one basic assumption. My first point of departure
is a question posed after I had delivered a paper with the
title "'Bridled Emotion': English Free Churchmen, Culture and
Catholic Values c.1870 - c.1945".[2] I was asked why I had given
no Baptist examples for my thesis. I replied that it might
have something to do with the basic distinction between Baptist and paedobaptist Free Churchmen: late Victorian paedobaptists, rediscovering, no doubt fancifully, their pedigree
as part of the church catholic, needed to express their fundamental unity in "catholic" buildings and liturgy; but for Baptists such yearnings were precluded by the radical nature of
Believer's Baptism. For Baptists the church was ever new; it
was a gracious discontinuity. For other Christians it was
more a matter of renewal; it was a redeeming continuity. Perhaps Believer's Baptism filled a need for Baptists which remained unfilled for Congregationalists, hence Congregationalism's search for St Francis and other protesting saints of
the church catholic. I would now want to modify that view,
although it retains certain charms.

My second point of departure is Geoffrey Rusling's sensible
booklet, *Baptist Places of Worship*: "Generally speaking ...
ours is not an inspired or an inspiring tradition in architecture". The author then affirms that a church building should
express the nature of God, the means He uses to address us and
which "He has provided for our approach to Him".[3] As to the
first proposition, generally speaking Geoffrey Rusling is
right. As for the rest, what could be more catholic?

My purpose, therefore, is to explore the interplay between
Baptist architectural inspiration and the inspiration behind
all church building, which is to enable God and man to meet
in the historic crisis of salvation. My basic assumption is
that Baptist architecture really does exist and not just architecture that happens to make do for Baptists. Indeed, it is
surprising how much architecture that happens to make do for
Baptists in fact proves to be *Baptist architecture*. It fits
the particularity of the situation. For those who remain un-
convinced of a Baptist response to architecture there is the
evidence provided by the *Baptist Handbook*, especially between
the 1880s and the 1930s.

In those years there were four chief types of response,
each illustrated in the *Handbook*. There were innumerable
instances of Baptists responding to Gothic, whether through
the competently starved Gothic of the Wesleyan Midlander,
John Wills, or the assured, comfy, endearingly arty crafty
Free Gothic of George and Reginald Palmer Baines. Then there
was the response to the institutional church, evident beyond
the call of duty in a series of hair-raising tabernacles:
Southport's Scarisbrick Road, "in the moresque style", onion-
domed above a semi-circular entrance;[4] or the "arch-round
Gothic" of Woodborough Road, Nottingham, its red tiled, rustic
roofed, clock faced tower standing octagonal guard ninety feet
above the junction of four roads;[5] or, beastliest of all,
Hayne of Frinton's Byzantine monsters, as if what politeness
repressed at Frinton could explode with propriety at West Ham
for Rowntree Clifford or at Clacton in memory of Archibald
Brown.[6] Such responses were the predictable outworkings of
the Nonconformist Conscience; but two other responses come
across with surprising strength. One is *churchliness*: that
is to say, the state of mind which builds a national *Church
House* in *Kingsway* faced in Baptist baroque, adjoining a chapel,
Kingsgate, faced in Baptist Wrenaissance.[7] The other response
is more complex, at once contradicting the churchliness, and
yet not always easily separated from it. This is a conscious
everyday architecture, here a Puritan meeting, there a people's
village church, sometimes a touch of public library or old
guild hall, sometimes lapping against the churchly, for is
Kingsgate Chapel more a bow to Sir Christopher Wren and St
Paul's or to Isaac Watts and Fetter Lane? But always there
is the determination to be woven into the fabric of the local
(or, in the case of Church House, the national) community.
The *Handbook* descriptions tell their own story: "A very plain
type of 'Queen Anne' ... with red brick facings, red brick
dressings, and green-slated roof" - thus Wallis Chapman's
Pembury Union Chapel near Tunbridge Wells, "the last chapel
in the building of which Sir Morton Peto took an active part".[8]
Or H. J. Capell's Leavesden, Hertfordshire, "well adapted for
a village, ... of the domestic Gothic type ... a pleasing and
picturesque group of buildings. The walls are of bright red
brick relieved by rough cast panels and stout timber studs".[9]
Or Healey's Cragg Chapel, Rawdon, between Leeds and Bradford,
classical "of the modified type that prevailed in this country
in the middle of the last century", and almost a chapel version
fifteen years early of Heathcote, Lutyens's famous suburban
villa at Ilkley.[10] In Leicestershire there was James Tait's
versatility. For Leicester's Clarendon Park Congregationalists
that meant fifteenth century Gothic, in random granite;[11] but
for the Baptists of Clarendon Hall it was "the popular Anglo-
Dutch style of the eighteenth century".[12] This was a style
ideally suited to "the requirements of a popular assembly".
It was cheerful, light, airy, convenient. "It readily lends
itself to all the practical requirements of present-day life
... and by its free and varied outlines gives a pleasing effect
without calling for any heavy or costly architectural features".
And you could hear in it, or at least its acoustic properties

were "unexceptionable".[13]   Clarendon Hall was for up-to-date
townees. At Kirby Muxloe, to suit a third the number, Tait
went for "English of the Tudor period, and of a rustic type";
"... a roof turret of picturesque outline, resembling the
ancient spires of Kent and Surrey [so suitable for the Shires],
help to give the building a distinct character as a place of
worship".[14]

So it continued in the next century. For Oldfield Park,
Twerton, in the Bath suburbs, and encouraged, perhaps guided,
by a cultured young minister, Silcock of Bath provided a chapel
"of eighteenth century character, in general accord with the
traditional Bath style ... The woodwork throughout is painted
white, and the walls are covered with a soft green paper, so
that a very quiet and pleasing effect is secured...". The
windows too were "of a slightly greenish shade".[15]   In Birmingham, at the Daniell Memorial Hall, Hope Street, Moseley, Silk
and Milton, of Ingall, Son and Milton, also went in for "a
bright-green stain... freely used, and it gives a cheerful
appearance, as the roof is stained dark-brown for contrast.
Most of the woodwork inside is treated similarly with green
stain. The style of the street front is a free adaptation of
modern Renaissance in bright red brick, with stone dressings";
and the front's chief features were two stone panels carved
with human figures clasping hands, expressive of the new age
of social fellowship and goodwill, a monumental treatment of
everyday Christian virtues.[16]   Bradshaw and Gass went public
library baroque at Farnworth, with red brick and grey terra
cotta "in Renaissance style".[17]   Arthur Keen crossed Cricklewood's Christopher Wrenaissance ("a freely-treated classic
style in red brick and stone, with green slate roofs", and
intersecting barrel vaults inside) with a Germanic tower and
belfry.[18]   Indeed, there is almost no end to it, but two further examples might be chosen to take the everyday theme
through the Great War and into the 1920s. The first is Hayne
of Frinton's Hutton and Shenfield Union Church, no monstrous
St Sophia this time, but an ancient guildhall "to harmonise
as far as possible with local conditions", half-timbered,
shingled and tiled.[19]   The second is Woking, by Thomas and
Jones of Swansea, "a Georgian type, following somewhat freely
the traditional style of building of the old Surrey and Berkshire towns".[20]

This is not quite selective history running out of control,
for these buildings have more than mere variety in common.
There is the everyday quality of neighbourliness, a response
to the traditions of the neighbouring community. There is
modishness; that is the message of the green stain. And
beyond the modishness there is the liberating effect of the
Queen Anne revival wherever it might lead; that is the message
of the red bricks, of the shades of Renaissance and Christopher Wrenaissance, of the movement into Georgian England. Between James Tait's Kentish mannerisms for a Leicestershire
village and Herbert Jones's old Surrey Georgian for new Surrey
Woking there is more architectural integrity, more purposive
evolution, than might at first appear.

So far the case is only partly made for Baptist architecture, although it has already been fairly made for architecture making do for Baptists. To make the case for Baptist
architecture, one must first turn to the practitioners.

That there were Baptist architects in the sense that there
were men, Baptists or not, who designed a host of Baptist
chapels, is clear. The firms founded by John Wills and George
Baines have already been mentioned. Their chapels, scattered
throughout England, together dominated the *Baptist Handbook*
for fifty years. The last Wills chapel, Attleborough, Nuneaton, was illustrated in 1931; the last Baines chapel,
Brighton Road, Newhaven, in 1938.[21] More interesting are the
architects, Baptist or not, who were reared in Baptist homes,
because some of these were pacesetters in their profession.
Sir Morton Peto is the spectre at every Baptist feast. One
of his sons, Harold Ainsworth Peto (1854-1933) was a fine
practitioner in his own right of the last flowering of English
landscape architecture on the grand scale. His partnership
between 1876 and 1892 with Ernest George was notably opulent.
Devotees of the Savoy Operas will rejoice that W. S. Gilbert's
town house should be by the younger son of a bold and bankrupt
Baptist baronet; the rest may marvel at George and Peto's
interpretation of Pont Street Dutch, the "wildly picturesque
Flemish burghers' houses"[22] of Collingham Gardens: but the
point is the red brick, burgher note for down-to-earth Sloane
Rangers and other everyday Kensington folk. Then there is
Alfred Gotch, two years older than Harold Peto, a nephew of
President Gotch of Bristol Baptist College, and "For many years
... the leading citizen of Northamptonshire". That is to say
he variously chaired the local Bench, Quarter Sessions,
Liberal Association and so on; and he was a dress reformer.
He was also a successful architect, the first provincial practitioner to be president of the R.I.B.A., with the then normal
successful specialism in country houses, banks, humane public
buildings and the like. Above all, Gotch was a pioneer architectural historian: *The Architecture of the Renaissance in
England* (2 volumes, 1891): *Growth of the English House* (1909);
Old English Houses (1925).

Their titles tell all; and the *Dictionary of National Biography* was quietly confident about Gotch's place in the canon:
"So thoroughly has Gotch covered the whole field that it is
unlikely that his work will be rivalled or outdated by any
other scholar".[23]

Norman Jewson is from a later generation, thirty years
younger than Gotch and Peto. As with Peto Baptist life was
more in his blood than in his line,[24] but his significance
for the present study is that he joined that group of craftsmen architects whose discovery of the Edwardian Cotswolds has
itself been rediscovered in the past decade. The nature of
their art is captured in the title of Norman Jewson's autobiography, now a collector's piece, *By Chance I Did Rove* and in
his *Times* obituary. Jewson and his friends were "realists
whose desire was to maintain the character of the English
countryside and its architecture and keep it alive and free".

They were men "whose hearts beat as one in their regard and
love for all that was finest in the English tradition" and
whose buildings, Jewson's in particular, "look as if they had
grown naturally from the ground".[25]

Some others of this group should also be noted here:
Ernest and Sidney Barnsley, the architect sons of a Birmingham
builder whose firm had several chapel committees among its
clients. Norman Jewson married Ernest Barnsley's daughter.
And there was Ernest Gimson. He was the son of a Leicester
engineer. The engineering Gimsons were secularists and it
was a lecture by William Morris to the Leicester secularists
which confronted Ernest with his vocation. But there were
also timber merchant Gimsons (like the timber merchant Jewsons)
and these were Melbourne Hall Baptists. Their kinsman, Ernest
Gimson, architect, furniture and plasterwork designer, more
successful than any of them in creating buildings which flowed
from nature and blended into it, was a charismatic figure.
It was his name which largely drew Norman Jewson to the Cotswolds, and their meeting was a turning point for Jewson. "I
felt that it had been the most wonderful and delightful day
of my life".[26]

For the moment Gimson and Jewson must be left there. They
will return, slantways, later. But what are we to make of
this?

Our first reaction must be one of scepticism, for what have
baptised believers to do with the immemorially earthy? The
testimony of a lapsed Methodist is pertinent here. In a novel
of 1935, *Introducing the Arnisons*, set at the turn of the century just when the Barnsleys and Gimsons and Jewson were
striking roots in the Cotswolds, Edward Thompson sends young
John Arnison and his friend Alan Thornhill to Grammond, a
Dissenters' boarding school somewhere in the Cotswolds. "Here
the past was all about them, with its voices and its hints of
memory. Leaning low, it whispered to them, and made them one
with a life and memory and tradition that are English of the
English".[27]

> It gave you roots in English soil; you heard the
> voice of past centuries. It was a bad education
> for the new age which was to be like Melchizedek,
> without ancestor or ancestral inheritance, and
> instead, broken off and new begun, and satisfied
> to be thus.
>
> Above all, I repeat, the Cotswolds are the wrong
> place for the education of a Methodist.[28]

The tension here identified between tradition and present
reality is at the root of the Protestant scheme of things,
which means that our second response must be compromise, for
the art of compromise is not to resolve tensions but to live
with them. Thus, we may explain, and perhaps dismiss, "Dissenting Gothic" as the (unfortunate) result of Protestant
Nonconformists living with tensions. Or we might go further,
for what we call "Dissenting Gothic" dissolves on examination,
as flimsy as the cast iron pillars which are its hallmark.

What we are really seeing is a "chapel" reflection of the pressing need for suitable buildings felt by all expanding sections of the increasingly complex Victorian community. Buildings say something, however contradictory, about their builders. Those builders, whether clients, craftsmen or professionals, do not live in a vacuum. They react to fashion, the sense of what is currently seemly and convenient and possible. In Victorian England especially there was an added factor which brought the tensions home, not least to Baptists: that was the growth of the building trade as big business and of architecture as a gentlemanly profession.

Building, architecture, and their sibling engineering, were the very occupations for parents to set young Baptists to over a matter of two or three generations, as Peto and Grissell, Peto and Betts, Higgs and Hill, and McAlpine, all testify. At some stage, usually where building or engineering swerve into architecture, taste must intervene, and then that other bright and representative young Nonconformist, that moraliser of taste, the mental art man, comes in: timber merchant turned designer, auctioneer turned estate agent turned architect, journalist turned architectural historian, mutual improvement society essayist turned suburban man of letters. Readers of Sylvia Legge's *Affectionate Cousins*, about the courtship of Marie Appia with the artist, poet and critic, T. Sturge Moore, will recall that the Moores were Tipple-ites, worshipping with the selectly cultivated church gathered by Samuel Augustus Tipple from the late 1850s at Central Hill, Upper Norwood, its interior "plain to bareness, but few buildings ... conveyed such a strange sense of worshipfulness", its minister "quietly beating out the music of his soul in public".[29] This is John Ruskin's South London a generation on and a little further out. But it is more than South London. Take Kettering's Alfred Gotch: his first cousin Francis Gotch was Waynflete Professor at Oxford, and his cousin Emily Hepburn married Josiah Whymper the engraver, and his brother Thomas Cooper Gotch was a major figure in the New English Art Club and the "Newlyn" school of artists, best known now for his "Holy Motherhood" (1902) in Newcastle's Laing Art Gallery. In the world of art, craft and culture, just as much as in the world of business, ministry and education, there are Free Church interconnexions.

So far my argument has been largely about chance, or *external* conditioning, about the sort of occupation to set young Baptists to; but with the mental art man, that moraliser of taste, we pass beyond chance or external conditioning, to recall the Free Church common denominator, that element which causes men to seek for *purpose*. The question of the *purpose* behind all this was asked, and frequently. Naturally the answer was in part a rationalising of current fancies and in part a distancing from them, a pacesetting to eternity. It could not have been otherwise, for such compromise is of the essence of theology, that most human of studies. From this point the present study's argument must become more purposeful.

Even Free Churchmen should trace the revival of English ecclesiastical architecture back to Pugin - all of it, including their share of it: High Gothic, Free Gothic, Arts, Crafts

and vernacular, splaying thence to Queen Anne and Renaissance
and so to the baroque, the classical and the Georgian. In
1847 the *Congregational Year Book's* sensible essay on chapel
architecture referred carefully but unambiguously to a correct
use of ecclesiological principles.[30] In 1850 the Wesleyan
F. J. Jobson's *Chapel and School Architecture, as appropriate
to the Buildings of Nonconformists* followed the ecclesiological
line with incalculable results for Methodist architecture,
perhaps for Methodism itself. Of all the English Protestant
mainstream, Baptists were least likely to be *shaped* by ecclesiological principles, but they too were bound to be affected by
them.

No doubt the prime inspirer of Baptist, as of most English
affections was John Ruskin whose *Seven Lamps* came out in 1849.
But there is much to be said for settling on Owen Jones, the
architect, and teacher at the South Kensington School of Design,
whose great opportunity came with his colour schemes for the
Crystal Palace and whose influential *Grammar of Ornament* appeared in 1856. Jones's book was not so much the poor man's as
the busy, nosey man's Pugin and Ruskin systematized: it was
possible to arrive at good taste; Nature provided the inspiration; the accumulated knowledge of the past disciplined that
inspiration into timelessly satisfying forms; the past included
the Orient, but it stopped short at the Renaissance. In his
dictionary of shape and colour, its element of artistic Grad-
grindery notwithstanding, Jones had provided his generation
with an Aladdin's Cave, or rather, a Crystal Palace.

Among those whom Jones impressed was Sir Morton Peto. Jones's
treatment was based on the belief that great ages in art re-
lied on the primary colours, notably blue. Peto's town house
in Kensington Palace Gardens was given the Jones treatment, as
were at least two of the neighbouring mansions and at least
one of Peto's Baptist chapels, Ladbroke Grove, Notting Hill,
opened in 1863, with a church formed in 1865, with James Archer
Spurgeon as its first minister. The Notting Hill Chapel received a mixed press. The minister's raptures were modified:
"I do not wish a better place inside; the only failing, certainly, is the outside". The minister's biographer is loyal:
"The style of architecture was thought at the time to be somewhat novel, the front being beautifully arched, while the interior was embellished in a style which some seemed to think
in advance of the times". It was done out in blue, gold and
white, or, as Peto put it, he had got "my good friend, Mr Owen
Jones, whose taste I admire so much, to do a little in the way
of ornamentation of the ceiling".[31]

This was early 1860s Kensington and Bayswater, six Baptist
chapels in the same neighbourhood with the seventh muscling in
because there were still "over 65,000 persons in the district
who cannot get into a Baptist chapel".[32] In 1869, six young
men, "whether Baptist or Independent", published *Religious
Republics: Six Essays on Congregationalism*. The fourth of
these was written by T. H. Pattison, minister of Rye Hill Baptist Church, Newcastle upon Tyne. His subject was "Congregationalism and Aesthetics".[33]

Of course Pattison was defensive ("there is a certain repressive power in our principles...") for his was "the perfectly righteous ambition", in the decade of *Culture and Anarchy*,
of the man "who takes broad and fair views of the purpose and
possibilities of his being", wishing "to live a life completer
and more melodious than ever the life of the mere agitator and
protester can be".[34] Pattison breathed the spirit of Jones. He
fought Matthew Arnold and Sydney Smith and the *Spectator*. He
annexed Dürer, Hogarth, Goldsmith, Fielding, Wordsworth to the
canon of Milton, Bunyan, Defoe, Robert Hall, John Foster. He
went further. "We have to build up for ourselves a life. In
our dilemma we turn back to the New Testament for precedents".[35]

We might not now be wholly satisfied with his exegesis but we
would still be struck by one element in his argument, which
is that Nonconformist baldness "may be in the most perfect
taste. It is true to our belief; it refuses to introduce
jarring elements. In this way we do homage to true aesthetic
laws. If in the churches of other communions the richest
symbolism is in keeping, in Nonconformist meeting-houses
there ought to be implicit trust in the power of simplicity,
from floor to ceiling, from porch to pulpit. Taking taste...
to mean that which satisfies... the requirements of our worship, I should say that there is ample scope for it... to
exercise a wonderful influence over our service".[36]

There was more yet: "The Congregationalist is to think for
himself, and to speak for himself, free from the bondage of
precedent; why should he not also design for himself?" "Besides, a chapel carefully thought out in design and substan-
tially executed in honest materials is a lasting proof of the
power of the Congregationalist system to clothe its principles
decorously and in suitable garb...".[37] This is an important
note because it introduces that sense of the value of the
vernacular, the *everyday*, which within two decades had become
the mark of Arts and Crafts. Pattison's stress is on the
common: "we aim at *common* worship"; the question of our architecture "especially commends itself to *the people*. *From
them* the designs for the chapel must come". Our needs are not
for precedent but for a building "in which *all* can see and *all*
can hear. To these two essentials all questions of style and
design ought to be subservient".[38] Thus a student of Ruskin
and Jones, perhaps of Pugin too, could by 1869 work through
Gothic to emerge the other side. "I believe that a refined
and well-educated Congregationalist must reject Gothic, just
because if it pleases his eye it will violate his convictions;
or if, on the other hand, it satisfies his principles and
demands, it must outrage his sense of beauty and harmony".[39]
As for Classical architecture, "What teaching is there for us
in classic plans or classic details?"[40]

Brave words for the 1860s, not least from the minister of
Newcastle's Rye Hill church, for his own premises had been rebuilt in that decade by a young man who was at once the most
sensitive, most articulate and most pronounced of Victorian
Dissenting Gothic architects. The young man was James Cubitt,
whose Nonconformist commissions, not least Rye Hill, illustrate

perfectly the tensions inherent in the search for a Nonconformist aesthetic, and the circularity of the chapel world.

     Cubitt is a shadowy figure, his articulateness notwith-
standing.[41]   His practice, which seems not to have been a
large one, extended from the 1860s to the 1900s. His best
buildings date from the 1870s and 1880s. Cubitt's was a
London practice, first at Finsbury Place, later at Broad
Street Buildings, but he had trained in the 1850s in both
the East and West Midlands, at Malvern and Nottingham, and he
had made a special study of the traditional church architecture of the East Midlands. His Nottingham master, J. C.
Gilbert, a man with a useful chapel connexion, illustrates to
perfection the world of the mental art man. One Gilbert
brother was an artist, another was the pioneer of the Rotham-
sted Research Station; Gilbert's mother was a Taylor of Ongar,
his father had been chairman of the Congregational Union; one
cousin was minister of the little chapel in Pembury, Morton
Peto's last; another was Medland Taylor, the fizzing Manchester church architect. The Howard Hintons were more distant
cousins; and two of the contributors to *Religious Republics*
were also cousins. When Cubitt later went into partnership
it was with a fellow pupil at Gilbert's, Henry Fuller. Today
Fuller is best celebrated as the architect of Clapton Park
Congregational Church, to many of whose leading members he was
related, and whose ancestry glowed with Baptist, Congregational
and Presbyterian Fullers, Berkshire farmers who banked, brewed
and practised their way through the middle ranks of generations
of the Dissenting better sort. Cubitt took over the practice
when Fuller retired in the 1870s.[42]

     Cubitt was surely a Dissenter, perhaps a Baptist. His
earliest works included Spurgeon's Stockwell Orphanage, begun
in 1867, and Spurgeon's Almshouses and Schools at Newington
Butts, but this connexion may simply have been brought about
by his work in the earlier 1860s for W. W. Pocock, whose best
theatre royal classical had landed the commission for Spurgeon's Metropolitan Tabernacle. Certainly Pocock's technical
achievements (and his drawbacks too) greatly impressed Cubitt,
for he referred to them in his essays; and it is in those
essays that Cubitt's particular significance lies. He contributed a series of papers on Chapel Architecture, Woodwork,
Cast Iron, and Recent Buildings, to *Building News*. He then
gathered much of this into two helpful and persuasive books,
*Church Design for Congregations: its Developments and Possib-
ilities* (1870) and *A Popular Handbook of Nonconformist Church
Building* (1892).

     Cubitt was an unabashed Goth. The contemporaries whom he
quoted with approval were all Goths: the younger Pugin, Butter-
field, Street, Burges, James Brooks, Seddon. So were his
sources, for which he pillaged Spain (Barcelona, and Gerona,
Pamplona and Salamanca), Middle Europe (Treves, Breslau,
Prague, Cologne), Romanesque France (Toulouse, Perigueux,
Angers, Bigorre), but also Byzantium (Trebizond, Ephesus,
Constantinople, Kieff, Thessalonika) and Italy in the shape of
Florence and Milan. Contemporary Edinburgh looked in; even
Wren did, because of his plan for St Stephen Walbrook; and

Cubitt's thirty-six printed sources included Pugin and Viollet le Duc. His goal was massive honesty and, mark of the true Goth, an historically grounded up-to-dateness which transcended mere fashion. For epigraph to *Church Design* Cubitt called Carlyle on *Heroes* to his aid. "We may say, the Old never dies till this happen, Till all the soul of good that was in it have got itself transfused into the practical New". Only thus could the best modern art best be joined to the best arrangement for modern purposes.

There was nothing anachronistic in Cubitt's concern for modernity. Given the choice he went to the thirteenth century for his inspiration because "our thirteenth century predecessors surrounded their own form of worship with an architecture as characteristic as it is grand - they would have devised an equally characteristic one for ours".[43] That was the point. "We cannot restore the old: we *may* transfuse what was good and permanent of it into the new".[44] For medieval man the nave was merely an outer court for the laity; "what was really held essential was what went on within - the work of the priests about the altar".[45] Well, for modern Protestant man what is really essential goes on all around him, for all are priests. Hence Cubitt's experimenting with the "magnificent capabilities"[46] of broad, columnless naves, great central crossings under a lantern tower, galleries only where the architectural shape allowed them. Hence his search for "breadth, space and largeness of parts", for an architecture which, "deprived of all adjuncts, can still assert its own power", an architecture which restores "attention to masses instead of edges, to gradated lights and shadows instead of lines", even to an intelligent play of imagination, "that endless change and mystery always inviting fresh study and promising fresh discoveries".[47] But though Cubitt was ever a Goth and shuddered at "the seventeenth century revolt against beauty", and though he had a particular horror of crimson cloth, "that lingering relic of the last century meeting house", the essence of his message, intelligently adapted, was bound to lead to a rediscovery of the crimson clothed meeting.[48] It is not fanciful to see this Puginite Puritan as an Arts and Crafts precursor, indeed, Gothic or not, as a companion to T. H. Pattison.

"The great charm of good architecture everywhere lies in this - that it expresses the aims and feelings of its founders: that centuries after they have passed away, it is still alive with their life...".[49]

The aims and feelings of the founders: that communal sense, indeed that common sense, that everyday sense given its proper dignity; "It is, after all, only with the intelligent concurrence of the public that architecture in these times can make any great movement".[50] A rarer sense accompanied this common sense, and that was a sense of the nature of Protestant worship, and the priestly unity of believers. "We may plan a grand open space before the pulpit and communion table, - surely a natural arrangement for a Protestant church".[51] That was where Cubitt's Gothic understanding tended.

So far the bulk of quotation has been from Cubitt's 1870
book. Any Art and Craft element is likely to be stronger
twenty years on. Then too the reference to the past, properly
understood, was no less insistent. "No preacher ... can be
always preaching; no poem can be always reciting itself; no
music can be always sounding in men's ears; but art is never
silent, its message repeats itself from century to century,
and there is no speech nor language where its noise is not
heard".[52] To build without art is "to get out of touch with
our contemporaries".[53] But there is now a new stress, liter-
ally an everyday stress for an age when "already we hear of a
future in which 'church work will have to be as varied as
human nature'".[54] There is an *organic* stress, as if already
form is following function as much in Cubitt's chapels as in
Louis Sullivan's Chicago banks. "The fact is, that the man
who does not give the first thought to the inside of his
buildings is not really an architect at all... In every design
worth calling such, the interior is the reason and motive for
the exterior".[55] And there is a *homely* stress: "Even the most
temporary, and cheapest, perhaps, of all architecture - that
of Japan - is genuine in its way".[56] "A church full of
thought and refinement will look respectable, whatever its
materials may be, and the secret of building well and cheaply
is just to use common materials in an artistic way... From
the common brick or rubble or tiles or concrete of the neighbourhood, something worth looking at may be made, if it is
only put together, as Opie said, 'with brains, Sir'".[57]
Cheap churches in everyday architecture must rely on picturesqueness, interest, individuality, on small slates or multi-
sanded tiles or brick dressings, a recreation of old English
architecture in its "wonderful variety and freshness".[58]
Cheap churches must, in short, be "their own best-selves -
realities and not reflections" - and cheap Nonconformist
church architecture especially deserves character, self-
reliance, individuality, those best qualities of the present
age.[59] "Let it only have courage to develop on its own lines,
to be itself... and the possibilities before it are very
great".[60]

This was a believer's architecture. Men "want to put something of their souls into their work, something of their aims
and hopes; they want the spiritual to shine through and trans-
figure the material. Where this is, there is art. It does
not depend on ornament, or luxury, or expense. The forms by
which it is expressed are a minor matter; its essence is the
appeal of mind to mind".[61]

And it was a Baptised Believer's architecure. For Cubitt,
as for all contemporary chapel architects, the Word was paramount, its paramountcy visible in the pulpit, audible in the
acoustics. But for Cubitt, at least, the sacraments were not
forgotten: the table and the baptistry. Cubitt did not like
to hide his baptistry under a rostrum. It should be an architectural feature, standing open, marbled and parapetted, oblong as in the catacombs, ideally placed where in a parish
church the altar should be, backed by a stone screen filled
with wrought iron grilles lest the congregation persist in

worshipping the organ pipes.[62]

So much for Cubitt's theory. Not too much remains of his
practice. His breakthrough was Congregational, first his
Emmanuel Church, Cambridge, in 1874, next his Union Chapel,
Islington, of 1876, with Dulwich Grove and West Kensington,
the former a vigorous scaling down of his original intentions,
the latter apparently in collaboration with J. M. Brydon,
both of them in the following decade. Of these four churches
it was Union Islington, built for Henry Allon and his people,
which marked Cubitt out. Cubitt won the competition, for
which Alfred Waterhouse was referee, under the pseudonym
"Torcello", for his design was inspired by Santa Fosca,
Torcello.[63] The requirements were demanding: a large congregation, an outstanding minister, a unique choral reputation.
They were accompanied by an architectural manifesto for what
must be at once and equally a preaching house and a worship
house, for a people hanging on the words *and* devotion of a
minister in turn dependent on them.

> Eloquence... is in the audience; the preacher's
> inspiration is not his theme only, but also the...
> kindling eyes and interested countenances of the
> people... The preacher may be loud in addressing
> an audience; he who prays cannot shout in addres-
> sing the Almighty... No hymn, chant, or anthem
> is sung in which the congregation does not join.
> The idea... in Union Chapel, is that the whole
> congregation shall sing from music-books in
> four-part harmony.

> The choir... is therefore only part of the singing
> congregation... in it, and of it - under no cir-
> cumstances separated from it... Our church
> buildings are for use, not for the realisation
> of conventional ideas.[64]

Torcello rose to the challenge: largeness of parts, shapes
and shadows, an intelligent mystery of counterpoint in arch
and column, at once monumentally confident and confidently
monumental. It is a great snail of a building, opened in the
presence of Mr Gladstone, hailed by one trade journal as "one
of the hundred remarkable buildings of the century", speaking
to one observer of "absolute congregational worship" and
costing, by the time the tower was completed, a dozen years
later, over £50,000.[65]

Union's spirit informed the rest of Cubitt's work, notably
Birmingham's Baptist Church of the Redeemer, Hagley Road,
opened in 1882 with Allon of Islington as a preacher, although
here the tower was a central octagon rather than a giant
pouncing on the passers-by of an inoffensive Georgian terrace.
The Church of the Redeemer (in careful contrast to the Unita-
rian Churches of the Messiah and the Saviour; it was nearly
called the Church of the Ascension) was marked by its great
lantern-towered central space, a galleried space, though
rumour persisted that this had run counter to the architect's
express wishes; and it was famous for its noble size, its
organ, and its draughts.[66]

Birmingham apart, Cubitt's best Baptist work was in Newcastle upon Tyne. Of his three Newcastle Baptist churches,
Rye Hill of the 1860s, Westgate Road and Jesmond of the 1880s,
only Westgate Road survives. In the 1880s an historic and
influential church, full of Anguses, left its Bewick Street
premises and divided to form two strategic new causes. The
larger one was at Westgate Road, opened in 1886; the smaller
one was at Osborne Road, Jesmond, opened in 1887.[67]

The Jesmond church was the more original, a Norman church
fitting into a long, narrow, wedge-shaped site between a main
road and a deep railway cutting. Cubitt was proud of its
acoustics, which were said to be "particularly good"; he was
also proud of his handling of an awkward site, because here
too the tower over the nave's middle point gave space, while
the device of a double transept gave breadth; and steps to
the chancel with its side choir stalls and open baptistry
led to the drama of Word and Sacrament. The breadth was
where it was needed most - near the pulpit. There was colour
too, for the chancel and baptistry were marble-paved in blue
and terra cotta against white. The widening nave, the steps
to the chancel, the arcading behind the baptistry, the colour
and texture of stone and marble, produced a sense of architectural movement whose impact reached its climax at baptismal services.[68]

At first sight there is little drama to Cubitt's church in
Westgate Road. It is unassuming, almost Dissenting Gothic.
Then the Cubitt strengths come into play: shape and shade,
three dimensional; texture, especially of the roof slates.
Inside there is breadth, restraint in decoration, an open
standing baptistry, a *congregational* dignity; and around there
laps the ancillary life of everyday Baptists in the large
windowed hall, the schoolrooms, the keeper's cottage, the
picturesque sense of medieval street that is conjured from
the narrow passage at the side of the church leading to the
cottage and the schools. Here certainly is the Goth on his
way to the Arts and Crafts.[69]

But there must first be a working out of the Gothic mood
with the apotheosis of Cubittism, although by a very different
kind of practitioner and for a very different kind of client.

The Thomas Coats Memorial Baptist Church, Paisley, of 1894,
is the most ostentatious of all the rich men's Dissenting
Cathedrals.[70] Beside its £110,000 and more of work Congrega-
tionalism's Albion, Ashton under Lyne, and its Leverhulme
churches in Bolton and the Wirral, pale. Coats Memorial was
built at the sole expense of Peter, Daniel and Archibald
Coats to the memory of the great thread manufacturer, Sir
Thomas Glen Coats. Their architect had already built the
Coats mansion at Ferguslie. Despite his name, Hippolyte Jean
Blanc, of The Neuk, Edinburgh, was Scottish born and bred,
the essence of the Scottish architectural establishment.[71]
He was a Tory politically, an antiquarian by inclination, with
a large practice in churches, mansions, public baths and halls,
libraries and hospitals, most notably the Edinburgh and Dis-
trict Lunacy Board's colony for a thousand patients at West

Bangour. When it came to churches, Blanc was a Goth, and
there was no lunacy about Coats Memorial. It is without doubt
a Cathedral, a Baptist St Giles, a bold appropriation of
France and Germany as well as Medieval Scotland, commanding
the hillside into which in fact it nestles, holding the whole
of Paisley in its view, upstaging every other Paisley church,
Paisley Abbey among them. Its completeness, from tiled
lavatories like reception halls to fonts in the vestibules for
drinking water (as opposed to stoups for holy water), from its
glass and carved screen to its pulpit and lectern, from the
ambulatory to the pews on runners to allow for easy cleaning,
is breathtaking. So is its colour, richly dimmed now, from
the vestibule mosaics to the chancel roof; so is the door
furniture, the hinges, the handles, the massive studs, the
niches in the stonework, so that when the outside doors are
opened wide they may fit into the walls despite their studs
and hinges and handles. That it is, as Blanc's obituary
claimed, "one of the finest examples of Gothic architecture
built in late years in Scotland",[72] cannot be gainsaid;
indeed, in conception it is a church on a Rockefeller scale.
But what might be overlooked in all the splendour is that it
is satisfyingly beautiful, and *that it works as a Baptist
church*. There is breadth, space and largeness of parts; there
are light and roomy and totally non-Gothic halls conveniently
beneath the church, adding grandly to its height, false base-
ments disguised rather than hidden from view by the Wagnerian
staircase rising from the carriage sweep to the suite of front
doors. In the main church people can see the preacher (and
hear him) and the table and the open baptistry. The choir is
side-stalled indeed, but it manages to be congregational, with
the organist seated behind what looks like an altar but is in
fact a console, facing congregation and choir alike, control-
ling them and choir alike. The vestries, generously chimney-
pieced, are meticulously equipped as baptismal changing rooms,
their period panelling folding out, rather as in an expensive
outfitter's.

For the purist the decorative eclecticism must be disturbing; the Gothic is not sufficiently free to be, if not ageless,
at least truly of its age. Yet the artistry of the transition
from antiquarian to Arts and Crafts, or slantways to Art
Nouveau, is not to be denied, a reminder that the Goth and
the Arts and Craftsman are to be seen in fruitful tension
rather than in conflict. Blanc, like Cubitt, was a scholarly
architect, as the titles of his occasional papers suggest:
"Medieval Abbeys: their Place as Schools of Art"; "The Arts
of the Monastery"; "Scottish Ecclesiastical Architecture in
the Fourteenth and Fifteenth Centuries". Blanc too was a
contributor to *The Builder*.

At this stage it is necessary to return to that most
eminent scholar-practitioner, Alfred Gotch, who in 1894, the
year of Coats Memorial, contributed an end paper on "Meeting-
house Architecture" to an *Album of the Northamptonshire Congregational Churches*. The subject embarrassed him. "No one
will pretend to find as much aesthetic interest in a meeting-
house as in an ancient church... built at a period when the

workman's mind spontaneously expressed itself in beautiful
forms". The trouble was that meeting houses had been forced
by political circumstances upon their people at a time when
"the workman's mind had ceased - or at any rate was ceasing -
to express itself in beautiful forms". It was a time, indeed,
when the craftsman was losing out to the architect and the
meeting house lost out to both. Yet, given his brief, and
finding what comfort he could in it, Gotch's message was predictable and clear: if architecture is not so much the art of
building nobly as "the expression in lasting materials of
those wants of man which grow out of and are connected with
the ever present necessity of shelter from the weather, then
we shall find a good deal to interest us in a survey of the
meeting-houses of the county". Gotch reflected that "if
anyone wishes to know what a fine chapel built in the reign
of Charles II would have looked like, he may gain a very fair
idea by visiting some of Sir Christopher Wren's city churches".
And he concluded that "True architecture will always express
the purpose for which a building is built, and so long as
the manner of conducting the services of the church and of
Nonconformist bodies differs so essentially as it does, so
long ought churches and chapels to carry the distinction on
their very faces".[73]

Here we back away from Coats Memorial, to return to the
message of Pattison or Cubitt carried to the stage where a
Kingsgate Chapel is as possible behind Kingsway's Church
House as a meeting is once more acceptable behind a village
green. But before this argument is pursued to a conclusion
there are some loose ends to be pulled together.

James Cubitt built both in Newcastle and Birmingham,
cities with a flourishing, indeed proud, local tradition of
architecture, indeed of craftsmanship. The donor of Cubitt's
Hagley Road site was William Middlemore, whose generosity
between 1848 and his death in 1887 made possible a string of
Birmingham Baptist Churches, several of them notable for their
size, their appointments and their worshipfulness. James
Cranstoun's spired Wycliffe, Bristol Road, of 1861, was said
in its day to be "the most beautiful Free Church place of
worship in the Midlands". Hamstead Road of 1883 and Oxford
Road of 1887 were equally spired.[74] If only because tasteful
buildings in eligible areas attract thoughtful congregations
who need ministers to match, it is possible to trace the impact of buildings on people through the sorts of men called
to their pulpits. There is an interconnexion of fabric as
well as of personality. For example the Hamstead Road Church
was known for its liturgical form of service (it used a service book) and its minister from 1899 to 1921 was one of the
Paisley Coats family, a Glasgow, Oxford and Leipzig sort of
man, "noted for fine culture of spirit as well as of intellect,
author of *Types of English Piety*".[75] The Middlemores, whose
largesse had made all this possible, were themselves a cultivated family. In the next generation the patronage of Thomas
and Theodosia Middlemore led to William Lethaby building a
distinguished country house for them at Melsetter, up in
Orkney. This is no more than to say that Midland Free Church-

men, regardless of denomination, were as likely as any other
Christians to benefit from Midland Arts and Crafts. The Methodists had Joseph Crouch (1859-1936), contemporary of Gotch
and Peto, in practice from 1884 to 1935, a man of gently modified consistency and gently radical social views, whose churchy
Wesleyanism, in line with F. J. Jobson, lies outside the present purview. Nonetheless, Crouch's published work adds to
the picture: *The Planning and Designing of a Methodist Church*
(Birmingham 1930); *The Apartments of the House* (1900); *Puritanism and Art* (1910) - this with an introduction by Silvester
Horne, the Congregationalist; *Churches, Mission Halls and
Schools for Nonconformists* (Birmingham 1901). Each volume is
a tribute in appearance and texture to the Arts and Crafts
gospel; so was each building, of which Baptists might note his
People's Chapel, Great King Street, of 1887, in firmly Arts
and Crafts Free Gothic.[76]   For the Congregationalists there
were the Bidlakes of Wolverhampton, father and son. The son,
W. H. Bidlake (1862-1938), was a Church rather than a chapel
architect, and may fairly be regarded as Birmingham's leading
Arts and Craftsman.[77]   The father, George Bidlake, was more
Dissenting Gothic than most of the practitioners so far mentioned.[78]   He was the author of *Sketches of Churches designed
for the use of Nonconformists* (1865), but he has a more immediate significance for the present study. A partner was James
Tait of Leicester, and a pupil, though only for a month, was
the young Philip Webb. Webb hated that month and "all that
God-forsaken prosperity drawn from terrible iniquity!"[79] But
Webb's brief Midland foray of 1854 is striking proof both that
here was a *trade* for bright young men, not yet redeemed into
a *craft*, let alone an *art*, and that a transformation was already in train, of tensions and reaction and movement.

Herbert George Ibberson (1866-1935) marks the transformation.[80]
He was a contemporary of the younger Bidlake and the Barnsley
brothers, a decade younger than Crouch, Gotch or Peto, a
generation younger than Cubitt or Blanc.

The Ibbersons were Fenland farmers and Baptists. Herbert
George was educated at Bishop's Stortford College from 1879
to 1882 and then trained to be an architect first at the Royal
Academy Schools, then in travel abroad, then in the offices of
a Reading firm and of the notable London architects, John
Belcher and J. D. Sedding. He practised in his own right from
1892 at Cambridge, in London at St Martin's Lane and Old Square
Lincoln's Inn, and in Hunstanton.

This was a suggestive training for an honourable career,
limited by ill health but marked by scholarship and public
spirit, a Gotch on a much smaller scale. The connexions cry
out for attention. Three London offices acted as outstanding
schools for Arts and Crafts practitioners: Norman Shaw's,
Ernest George's, and J. D. Sedding's, the last of these given
added flair by the junior partner, Henry Wilson, who was
Ibberson's contemporary. It was at Sedding's office that
Ibberson came across Ernest Gimson and Alfred Powell who were
his fellow pupils. Barely a generation later Ibberson's own
pupils included his kinsman, Norman Jewson. It was through

Ibberson that Jewson first heard of Gimson and saw photographs
of his cottage architecture which convinced him of Gimson's
"superiority to all other living architects whose work I
knew".[81]

The stage is thus set for a connexion of commissions, frequently Free Church, whether domestic, institutional or ecclesiastical, all of them a sensitive everyday architecture, with
a particular quality of texture. Of Ibberson's domestic work,
the best example is Raenstor Close, the Derbyshire house
above Bradford Dale, which he built between 1908 and 1910 for
the Misses Melland, the daughters of a rich, Liberal, Congregational, Manchester cottentot turned bleacher and banker.
The Mellands were returning to their ancestral dale, hence
their almost manor house, Orpheus carved on its gateposts,
suggestive of the ladies' musical talents, the zodiac in
plaster on the drawing room ceiling, suggestive of an architect's whim, the wax polish, the carefully informal gardens,
the picturesqueness of shape and purpose. Of Ibberson's institutional work there are two houses and a class room block
built for his old school, Bishop's Stortford, between 1909
and 1914, and there is what Pevsner describes as a "specially
nice" gymnasium, also of 1914, for Homerton College, Cambridge, gentle buildings each with Ibberson's special mannerism of brick inset with flint.[82]

The house, the school, the college, were all for Free
Churchmen; but it is in Ibberson's churches that one learns
most about him. Ibberson was a Baptist who married a Congregationalist. By then he had settled with others of his
family at Hunstanton where they busied themselves at Union
Chapel, a rather starved Gothic building, outwardly unexceptionable, of 1871. But the Ibbersons transformed the interior,
and they did so through the agency of Herbert George. They
gave the organ and the communion chairs; theirs, or rather
his, was the spirit of symbolism that pervaded the place:

> Each hymn-board... proclaims a truth about hymn-
> singing. At the top of the board on the left of
> the congregation there is carved an ill-nourished
> bird; one of its legs is broken, and its wings
> hang helplessly down; it is surrounded by dying
> leaves and rose petals and above is the cross of
> suffering. Yet the bird still sings, and across
> the face of the board are the Latin words -
> *Dolens Lauda*: when in sorrow, praises. There are
> arrows among the leaves, but they are only remin-
> iscent of St Edmund, the patron saint of Hunstanton.
>
> The bird at the top of the other hymn-board is
> well-favoured and uninjured; roses and rose-leaves
> in full beauty are surmounted by a crown of triumph
> and the bird is in full song; *Gaudens Lauda* is the
> message - when rejoicing, praises.[83]

From 1895 to 1899 Union's minister was a Spurgeon's College
man of Cotswold farming stock, Wyndham Colin Bryan (1858-1919).
In 1888 Bryan had married Caroline Jewson, who was at once

Herbert Ibberson's cousin and his sister-in-law; she was also
Norman Jewson's aunt. Bryan was especially sensitive to the
"beauty, dignity, and orderliness both of places of worship
and acts of worship" and he both encouraged and influenced
Ibberson. When Bryan moved from Hunstanton to Rickmansworth,
where he ministered from 1899 to 1911, he ensured that Ibberson
should design the mission cause which he was promoting at
Chorleywood; and again at Ampthill between 1911 and 1913 he
got Ibberson to do his best to beautify the interior of an
unyielding building.[84]

The work at Chorleywood is of particular interest.[85] Bryan
had been offered the site and £200 by a local developer, who
was a Baptist. In April 1905 the stone was laid of the first
phase of the new chapel complex. By September, which was when
the building's first phase was completed, nearly £1200 had
been raised. Within three years the debt was paid off. Mean-
while, in 1906 Ibberson had exhibited at the Royal Academy a
design for the complete building, a grandly Free Gothic church,
rather in the manner of Sedding's partner (and Ibberson's contemporary) Henry Wilson. It was to have a great Gothic west
window deepset under an arch between massive buttresses; it
was to be gargoyled and picturesquely roofed in the everyday
of Scotland or England or parts of Germany, it is not clear
which. The building would come to life in the contrast between
the plain, massy walling and the picturesque roofing. The
building which actually appeared, however, nestling long, low
turreted under the brow of a hill in a Chiltern landscape of
woods and little valleys whose contours still preserve it outwardly from the insistent thickening of surburban housing, was
to be the church hall. It is a cement rendered building,
grey-green slated, its windows gently arched, and mullioned in
Monk Park stone. It commands attention for four reasons: its
style, its texture, its fittings and its name.

Its style has led its most recent historian into the very
plausible speculation that it was influenced by Charles Voysey
who had lived at The Orchard, just up the hill from the church,
since 1900. Voysey's buildings are full of mannerisms used in
Ibberson's chapel: the horizontality, the materials, the
colouring, the mass of roof sweeping down to the overhanging
eaves, flaring out into a "bell cast finish" protecting the
walls and windows "in a typically Voysean manner".[86] The fur-
nishings and fittings too are Voyseyesque - the piano stool,
the communion chairs, "part Voysey, part country",[87] the vestry
fireplace, the Japonaiserie of darkwood strips against white
walls: at least, it is "commercialised Voysey",[88] for this
almost sensuous mingling of texture and design, structural
material and ancillary fittings, is Arts and Crafts shading
into Art Nouveau in a way which neither Voysey nor Ibberson's
master Sedding could have approved. It is in everyday, visual,
textured, materials - yellow stock bricks, rough cast gables,
grey green slates, golden brown mullions, untreated oak doors,
red clay tiles fitted into the ventilator openings (this was
an Ibberson mannerism used at Bishop's Stortford), buttresses
with a brick and flint chequer design (another Ibberson touch,
used at Homerton); and inside a wide room in white, yellow and

blue, red brown pine herringbone tiles on the floor and round
the walls a dado of panels in tapestry, velvet and faience,
deep blue and dark green, framed in dark pine, an architectural
use of colour and fabric dashingly rare in Free Churches. Are
these materials or fittings? The distinction is hard to make,
and it is here that Ibberson comes into his own.

At Union Hunstanton he went to town with fretted heart
motifs on the roof truss and communion table, with Art Nouveau
tendrils in the stained windows, with repoussé copper plaques.
The same enthusiasm wisps and bubbles at Chorleywood,
coloured and textured and shaped, delicately understated. "I
am the Door", says a Greek inscription flanked by vine leaves
on a repoussé lead panel above the entrance. "My House shall
be called the House of Prayer" is carved above the porch.

The entrance is low; the hall beyond it is high and light
and broad. The effect is consciously artful. Above the curve
of the arch that backs the communion platform, and carefully
lit from behind, hangs a hand made copper cross with repoussé
designs. There are windows with blue green designs of nails,
the crown of thorns, a heart; there are crosses again and a
Calvary scene and more green and blue in the circular west-
end gable window. The designs are stylised; the glass by
virtue of its type and colour has a liquid quality. There are
bird and leaf motifs on the roof trusses, and, until they were
insensitively replaced, there were homely chairs, not pews,
rush seated, in natural beech and oak and pine.[89]

The building was certainly simple and cheap, though there
was nothing cheap about the masterly quality of the brickwork
round its doors, and as a concept it was sophisticated, even
complete for all that it was never finished. Here was artistry
nowhere quite slipping into artfulness, genuinely everyday because this vernacular could not escape the suburban civilisation which had given the cause birth and which nourished its
congregation. As the *Builder's Journal* put it, "The building
committee... desired to make no attempt with the thousand
pounds at their disposal to imitate the glories of a parish
church".[90] That was the point. At least until the main
church was built, which it never was, this was to be - and
to be called - a Meeting House; and when in 1934, at the end
of Ibberson's life, a gift of £3500 enabled the congregation
to build church halls and caretaker's rooms, with Ibberson as
architect, they maintained what had become the tradition,
yellow brick, handled with mastery, grey green slates, tiles,
the whole so domestic and understated that it is hard to
realise quite how good it is.

There is no large Ibberson church, but there is one which
fits between the meeting at Chorleywood and the church which
it was intended to grow into, and that is the Congregational
(now United Reformed) church at Elmers End, opened in 1930.[91]
Elmers End is almost in Kent, just as Chorleywood is really
in Hertfordshire, and although Elmers End was Congregational
and Chorleywood was Baptist, both were, as was said of Elmers
End, union churches "in fact and in practice".[92] Elmers End
too is an unfinished essay in texture and colour: Sussex

grey wealden bricks, golden brown slates, Milton and Bunyan
in Ham Hill stone each side of a deeply recessed great west
window, a benched forecourt garden for the weary, and simple
low doors with "Come unto me all ye that labour" carved over
them in oak; and a lofty interior, acoustically difficult,
barrel vaulted, walls rough cast in yellow plaster, woodwork
almost black, the whole illuminated by bowls held by angels
casting the light up to the ceiling. That was Ibberson's idea.
So was the introduction of fabric, a "fall of sky-blue damask
of great height" behind the table under a canopy of blue and
gold bearing the Latin words *Jesus Hominum Salvator*: I.H.S.

Ibberson explained it all enchantingly in his brochure, his
lightness of tone not really hiding the passion of his principles, his love of light and touch, his determination to
prove that a building "almost violent in its stark austerity"
yet could be "cheerful, even gay":

> And then on 'Communion Sunday', let the table be
> brought down from its high place, cover the cloth
> of gold with plain linen, gather around it as a
> family in simple fellowship and remembrance, and
> so by the very change of position emphasize our
> Protestant Faith.

The table was Protestant, but catholicity lay defiantly in the
Latin words, *Jesus Hominum Salvator*. What Greek was to
Spurgeon, Latin seems to have been to Ibberson.

> I know Latin has a sinister suggestion, calling up
> obscurantism and cruel things. But it's a fine
> sonorous tongue, it's dead, so it can never die or
> be corrupted, even by America. And it is the only
> universal tongue. If a Briton [sic] peasant peddling
> onions looks through an open door, he will understand
> - and the Italian organ-grinder, or the Bavarian
> cornet-player in a German band, and the public school
> boy from - anywhere. All will know what 'Jesus
> Hominum Salvator' means. And it will link all to-
> gether, Quaker, Catholic, Baptist, Independent,
> Unitarian. Jesus is the Saviour of man to them all,
> though as to *how* they are saved they may all differ,
> and perhaps none understand.

> Outside, the gable stands up high among the friendly
> little houses... Bunyan and Milton guard the Free
> Church (Congregational) principles. The symbol of
> the Church invisible stands in the great window, a
> Cross, vacant and made joyous with gold for 'He is
> risen'.

> Under the arch of the entrance is carved 'Come unto
> me all ye that labour' - I expect that 'labour' will
> be held to mean suffering as well as work. I am sure
> that the poor will always be welcome, and I trust
> that even the rich will not be sent empty away.[93]

It is hard to know when or how to cease quoting advocacy of
such charm, the more so because there cannot be many examples

of an architect, at once "an artist to his finger-tips, and
a Free Churchman to the marrow of his bones", explaining the
wholeness of a profession which is to him almost a vocation.[94]
When Ibberson died, suddenly despite his long ill health, an
appreciation dwelt on this aspect of him.

> He was a Puritan mystic [there were many such in
> the 1930s]. I remember once sitting with him in
> one of our typical chapels of the 'Nonconformist
> Doric' period, square and ugly. When I remarked
> that it was like an old barn, he turned on me.
> Said he, 'An old barn may be one of the most
> beautiful buildings on this earth. I would not
> exchange some of this for any of the sham Gothic
> places, with their pretentious vulgarity.[95]

Here at last the scholar architect, child of the Gothic
liberation, confronted with meeting house vernacular, has
worked himself out of the remaining prejudices, the original
sin, implanted by the Gothic revival. He is too good a pro-
fessional not to be alert and responsive to the proper pressures of fashion, and too good an artist to desert principle.
The tensions that I have traced throughout this study are in-
eradicable; they exist in him, but there has been some movement into a largeness of vision. Perhaps Ibberson was Gotch's
master builder, banished since the seventeenth century, an
artist craftsman building at last for his sort. That Ibberson
understood his clients and warmed to them is beyond doubt, as
two necessarily lengthy quotations, the first more frivolous
than the second, might suggest.

Ibberson's ecclesiastical clients were an eclectic bunch of
Baptists, Congregationalists, Anglicans, Roman Catholics and
Christian Scientists. He had the measure of them:

> The Spirit of the Lord is with all these people, but
> their ways are strangely different. I am thinking
> of writing a tract on 'Comparative Committees'. The
> Baptists are great on teas; we lay stones with teas
> and open with more tea. The Vicar is roped in, with
> the chairman of the local council, and representatives
> of sister churches. Mrs Eddy had none of these
> material rejoicings, so her followers have none;
> nothing happens at the beginning or the end, except
> the usual 'testimony meeting'; no public thanks to
> builder or architect. But they wrote to me, officially,
> charming letters of thanks, not only at the end, but
> in the middle of the work.[96]

The second quotation speaks for itself. It is a letter
written on the "Train to Town", 13 August 1917, to his kinsman
Frank Bryan, one of W. C. Bryan's two minister sons and at the
time minister at Hope Chapel, Cowbridge Road, Cardiff, and
bravely taken with the idea of rebuilding Hope.

Dear Frank,[97]

That a Nonconformist minister is interested in
architecture, always rejoices my heart, that one
tries to think it out on scientific lines has for
me the delight of novelty - I'm new to it myself.

The idea of getting a ritual (and in a way a doctrine) which shall make people - accustomed to
fight like cats - bill and coo as turtle doves,
is of course 'in the air' - you get it with Orchard
and Malcolm Spencer.[98] (Spencer needs it in his
home - do you know his wife? a high Anglican
'worker' delighting in retreats to nunnerys and
all that pertain to altars!) I think you have it
too so long as you *keep what we have got intact.*

Well about the house for the faith.

I feel that we must insist on the holding up of
the Lord in the sermon as very important, the
modern man will more and more be accessible through
his brain. This means you must see and hear well -
largely rules out domes which are acoustically bad,
and pillars which hide the fair face of the minister.
Pillars and arches which merely cut off the gangways
are all to the good. The difficult thing for me is
what are our people to *look* at besides the minister.
On the whole I don't think we can run to a chancel,
we do not want a *sacred* screened off place for the
altar and its ministrants, where our Lord can be
'made and eaten all day long' - and to shut up a
lot of women in hats in a starved and skimped apse
has no reasonableness in it - Neither do I care to
seem to worship pipes.

I, in my present mood would carry the roof for its
full height and width right on - but put the pulpit
on one side and the organ on the other (or both) and
have a great cross on the end wall, or a fresco of
the resurrection. For thoughts come through the eye
though less so than through the ear. Of course you
can have a window, but windows properly treated are
not very easily read, and I prefer strong light from
the sides on a picture or emblem. I do not care for
the table dead on the end wall - it is not for us an
altar of sacrifice. I like your idea of the marble
pool of baptism at the end, but it should be dominated
by the Cross which belongs to us all...

As you say we have, or ought to have, the family
feeling, but at the same time we ought to want [?]
the feeling of awe in the presence of supreme love
- If possible we should get it in two buildings -
The church should not encourage conversation or
thoughts of the details of one's neighbour's life,
but the Hall should encourage both. The hall should
be a great place in our life and all that the tea
meeting stands for should be run for all its worth,

and so should the prayer meeting. In getting all
we can from the catholics we must not lose what
belongs to us especially - as you say in getting
to grasp the idea of *the* church we must not lose
the idea that we are *a* church -

When you can have only *one* building things are more
difficult - After the war I hope to be up against
the problem of a school hall at B.S.C.[99] which will
be also a school chapel - It must be solemn enough
for communion services, gay enough for a school
chantey - ('with a yo heave ho and a cheer for little
Polly...!')

I'm thinking there of putting my communion table
(and Cross if I can get it) in a recess under the
organ, and to cover it with a gay curtain when
social life is to the fore. I shall get plenty of
light into the building and decorate largely in
white which is both cheerful and solemn.

Going back to the plan, this is of course influenced
by the site, in some cases the octagon type is more
satisfactory. Horton's[100] is good and, for a wonder,
his great vault, like a dome, has no echo.

I've an open mind as to 'style'... Gothic is fairly
flexible and I rather lean to it, so long as you do
not let the domanant [sic] past make you a copyist.
The Renaissance is good too, so long as one isn't
carried away under its influence to the pride of
life. For quite little places 'Jordans' is a
charming jumping off place.[101]   I'm personally fond
too of the Italian Romanesque stuff, rather simple
round arches, but with delicate late work in the
fittings - but we must whatever we do steer between
the rocks of pedantic copying and the whirlpool of
striving to be 'original' - we must let practical
requirements and the ideas of our worship dominate
us - in the spirit which giveth life.

All this is written dogmatically, but I am really
only, as you are, feeling my way - and naturally
with a greater sense of its difficulties than you
can have.

I was spending the night at Malcolm Spencer's last
week and talked Architecture a little. He is interested in architecture a good deal chiefly I
think under his wife's influence and his mind runs
most in details - how far can we have something
which looks like an Anglican altar, and should we
call family prayers 'Compline'. This rather to
propitiate the Catholics with whom his gracious
soul longs to be in harmony, than because they form
part of a scientifically thought out scheme of
architecture and ritual as a development of
'nonconformity' - (horrid expression).

Well good bye.   I'm going to read about Henderson
his resignation.[102]

Thine H.G.I.

Of course I've been thinking thro' this of Chorley
Wood Chapel, and your father - I'm sure he is interested in the subject of building churches and I
know (only too well) he is in *me* so perhaps you
might send this letter on to him.

Wyndham Bryan was dead within two years and Frank Bryan's
Hope, Cardiff, was not rebuilt in his time there or by Ibberson,
although when the new Hope did take shape, twenty years on, its
Franciscan facade fitted Ibberson's fondness for the "rather
simple round arches" of the Italian Romanesque; he would have
warmed to the gentle colouring of its brick and tiles and Portland stone dressings and to the interior severity of the large,
bare, oblong room for worship.[103]   The new Hope's architect,
Ivor Jones, was not a Stortfordian, although he was an Old
Millhillian. And ill health took Bishop's Stortford College's
Memorial Hall from Ibberson too; his plans were abandoned and
a very different, more flambuoyant building was put up on a new
site by Clough Williams Ellis.

What nearly began with Geoffrey Rusling should almost end
with him. "Whether we recognise it or not, the building we put
up is going to say *something* about us and it is going to do
something to us".[104]   Not even Baptists, it seems, can get away
from mere appearances and Geoffrey Rusling joins James Cubitt,
Alfred Gotch, Herbert Ibberson and every other thinking architect or architectural commentator. Indeed, he joins the human
race for we are all of us architectural commentators to the
extent that we express ourselves about what encloses our particular space. But Rusling has more to say: "The only true basis
for church architecture is a biblically grounded theology of
worship and a building committee which began its work with a
course of study groups on this subject would be starting in a
most enlightened manner".[105]

Those who champion the engagement of all the senses in our
worship, of touch and drama, sight and movement, will sigh at
this retreat from celebration to cerebration. The Word, once
confined to our pulpits, has been released - for our study
groups. Others, however, will recognise the arts and crafts
spirit, the striving in a fallen world for understanding in
communion with practice. "The care we give to our churches
while they are being shaped in committee discussion and on the
architect's drawing board will itself be an act of worship".[106]
Rusling is right. Eighty years on he has caught the spirit of
James Cubitt's Westgate Roaders up in Newcastle. "Night after
night", so one of them recalled in the 1930s of the atmosphere
of the 1880s, "they pored over architect's plans and specifi-
cations, and so thoroughly did they master the details that,
before the walls arose, one of them said, 'I can already walk
in and out of the building!'"

"Day by day they watched the progress, spending a little
time there on going to or returning from business... I asked

if the beams in the roof were to be stained or varnished, only
to be told that age would give them the necessary tone, and I
laid the lesson to heart".[107]

So back to Rusling. Church buildings, he reminds us, should
express the nature of God, the means He uses to address us and
which He has provided for our approach to Him.[108] There we
have that deceptive simplicity which is the essence of Puritan
architecture: all that has to be done is so to enclose a space
that that space is liberated for its best use, which is His
people's approach to God. The problem is reduced to three
syllables: Does it work? That is the craftsman's problem.
Where it is solved, art results.

NOTES

1 C. H. Spurgeon, *Autobiography* Vol.2. *The Full Harvest 1860-1892*,
   Banner of Truth edition 1973, pp.11-12.

2 C. Binfield, "'Bridled Emotion': English Free Churchmen, Culture and
   Catholic Values c.1870 to c.1945", in A. C. Duke and C. A. Tamse eds.
   Britain and the Netherlands, Vol.vii, *Church and State Since the
   Reformation*, The Hague 1981, pp.176-206.

3 G. W. Rusling, *Baptist Places of Worship*, 1965, pp.3,6.

4 By E. W. Johnson of Southport. *Baptist Hand Book (BHB)* 1893, p.285.

5 By Watson Fothergill. "There is rather a novel feature about the
   baptistery, in that there is a passage into the dressing rooms through
   a door beneath the pulpit, and therefore no need for candidates to
   ascend into the open chapel'. *BHB* 1896, pp.312-4.

6 For Frinton see *BHB* 1912 p.514; for the West Ham Central Mission see
   BHB 1915 p.484, 1923 p.298; for Archibald Brown Memorial Clacton see
   BHB 1923.

7 A. T. Ward, *Kingsgate Chapel*, 1912, *passim*; *BHB* 1940 p.351.
   C. Binfield, "English Free Churchmen and a National Style", in S. Mews
   ed. *Religion and National Identity: Studies in Church History* Vol.18,
   Oxford 1982, p.532.

8 *BHB* 1888 p.342; 1890 p.364.

9 *BHB* 1889 p.382.

10 *BHB* 1892 p.358 f.

11 *Congregational Year Book (CYB)* 1887 pp.256-7.

12 *BHB* 1893 p.290. It was to hold 1000, and its plan was "somewhat in the
    form of a Latin Cross".

13 Ibid.

14 *BHB* 1897 p.315.

15 The minister was the Revd B. Oriel, who "led" his people to a good
    building (ruined nonetheless by its tip-up seats). I am grateful to
    the Revd Dr L. Champion for this recollection. *BHB* 1904 p.401.

16 *BHB* 1907 p.487; I am grateful for further information from the Revd
    Bessie Selwood.

17 *BHB* 1907 p.488.

18 *BHB* 1908 p.509. A Greek Cross plan to hold 800. "The interior effect will depend mainly on two great barrel ceilings, richly decorated and intersecting each other over the central area".

19 *BHB* 1914 p.509.

20 That is to say, silver grey bricks, bright red brick quoins, arches and string course, Bath stone dressings. *BHB* 1928 p.324.

21 *BHB* 1931 p.336; 1938 p.364.

22 The phrase is Mark Girouard's, *Sweetness and Light*, Oxford U.P. 1977, p.224.

23 *Dictionary of National Biography* sub Gotch, John Alfred, 1852-1942.

24 "My Father's family were Baptist [and] he never went to church except for weddings and funerals". Miss Nancy Jewson to author, 24 January 1980.

25 *The Times*, 10 September 1975.

26 N. Jewson, *By Chance I Did Rove*, privately published, 1973, p.15.

27 E. Thompson, *Introducing the Arnisons*, 1935, p.43.

28 Ibid. p.248.

29 Sylvia Legge, *Affectionate Cousins: T. Sturge Moore and Marie Appia* Oxford U.P. 1980, pp.34-5; A. Porritt, *The Best I Remember*, 1922, pp.4-5.

30 "Remarks on Ecclesiastical Architecture as Applied to Nonconformist Chapels", *CYB* 1847, pp.150-163, esp.pp.152,161-2.

31 G. Holden Pike, *James Archer Spurgeon DD, LLD*, 1894, pp.77,72,74.

32 Ibid. p.77.

33 T. H. Pattison, "Congregationalism and Aesthetics", *Religious Republics: Six Essays on Congregationalism*, 1869, pp.133-168.

34 Ibid., pp.133,143,142.

35 Ibid., p.145.

36 Ibid., p.148-9.

37 Ibid., p.160, 163.

38 My italics; Ibid. pp.147, 162, 159.

39 Ibid. p.160.

40 Ibid. p.160.

41 I am indebted for information about Cubitt to Mr J. Bettley, of the library of the R.I.B.A.; and to Mr Neil Burton of the Greater London Council, Historic Buildings Division. Cubitt's dates were 1836-1912.

42 I am indebted for information about Henry Fuller to Mr J. Bettley, and to Mr A. A. Smith.

43 J. Cubitt, *Church Design for Congregations: Its Developments and Possibilities*, 1870, p.7.

44 Ibid. p.105.

45   Ibid. p.7.

46   Ibid. p.19.

47   Ibid. pp.95, 57, 39-40, 61.

48   J. Cubitt, *A Popular Handbook of Nonconformist Church Building*, 1892, pp.27,30.

49   Cubitt, *Church Design*, p.8.

50   Ibid. p.v.

51   Ibid. p.19.

52   Cubitt, *A Popular Handbook*, p.4.

53   Ibid.

54   Ibid. pp.4-5.

55   Ibid. p.17. In this connexion, Cubitt's fascination with Byzantine architecture is of particular interest: perhaps his mentor in this was Burges, perhaps it came from more general observation. Among Cubitt's examples in *Church Design* was St Sophia, Constantinople, a building whose exterior has little appeal, or sense, unless understood as its interior turned inside out. This is the climate of thought which made Bentley's Westminster Cathedral not just possible but profoundly influential.

56   Ibid. p.26. Again a curiously suggestive, and perceptive comment.

57   Ibid. p.27.

58   Ibid. p.75. Or, if brick, a recreation of the late Gothic and Renaissance of the Netherlands and East Anglia, Ibid. p.74.

59   Ibid. p.28.

60   Ibid. p.74.

61   Ibid. p.121.

62   Ibid. pp.104-5; 49.

63   I am grateful to Mr N. Burton for this information.

64   W. Hardy Harwood, *Henry Allon, D.D., Pastor and Teacher*, 1894 pp.55-8, also quoted in Cubitt, *Popular Handbook* pp.2-3,67-8.

65   Harwood, op.cit., pp.61,68.

66   Its total cost was £17,340. See T. W. Hutton, *The Church of the Redeemer, A History 1882-1957*, Birmingham 1957, pp.2-16; J. M. Gwynne Owen, *The Chronicles of Our Church*, Birmingham, 1902, pp.73-86.

67   See *Westgate Road Baptist Church: Jubilee Handbook*, Newcastle-upon-Tyne, 1936, passim; and *Handbook*, 1904, p.60. The Rye Hill church, formed 1817, was rebuilt by Cubitt c.1864. By 1901 the congregation had removed to a new site, Wyclif, Elswick Road, designed by George Baines. (*BHB* 1901 p.358). The Rye Hill premises became a People's Theatre and then a clothing factory. I am grateful to Mr R. Wilson for elucidating the history of Rye Hill.

68   Cubitt, *Popular Handbook*, p.49; I am grateful to Mr J. Trevor Williams for information about the Jesmond Church.

69   And in 1898 Cubitt charmingly bowed to the Arts and Crafts inevitable

with his pretty infant school for Loughton's Union Chapel in metropolitan Essex. With its red brick walls, its tiled roof, its half-timbered gable and porch in English oak, and its wooden casemented windows, it was a natural subject for T. Raffles Davison, that most persuasive of the Arts and Crafts movement's architectural artists. "The general treatment is that of seventeenth century domestic work". *CYB* 1899, p.153.

70 *BHB*, 1895, pp.296 ff.

71 For Blanc (1844-1917) see *The Builder*, 30 March 1917, p.206.

72 Ibid.

73 J. A. Gotch, "Meeting-house Architecture", T. Stephens ed. *Album of the Northamptonshire Congregational Churches*, Wellingborough 1894, pp.159-60.

74 A. S. Langley, *Birmingham Baptists Past and Present*, n.d.c. 1939 *passim*, esp. pp.90-1, 85; 117,144.

75 Ibid. pp.118-9.

76 For Crouch see *Journal*, R.I.B.A., May 1936 p.768; *Birmingham Post*, 4 April 1936; for The People's Chapel see *BHB* 1897, p.304.

77 See S. Webster, "W. H. Bidlake 1862-1938", *West Midlands Architecture*, No.26 June 1976 pp.17-25.

78 He was in practice from c.1849; he was the architect of several Midland Congregational Churches, most notably Abbey Foregate, Shrewsbury (1862) and Queen St., Wolverhampton (1864). He was the architect of Tettenhall College (1865), the Free Church boarding school, and a governor of it; the builders of the College were John Barnsley and Sons.

79 James Tait (1835-1915) was a pupil of G. G. Scott, a kinsman of William Burges and, distantly, through his wife, of the Adam brothers; his father was a Leicestershire Congregational minister. I am indebted to Mr D. A. Barton for this information. W. R. Lethaby, *Philip Webb and his Work*, 1979 ed., pp.10-11, 235.

80 I am indebted for information about Ibberson to the Revd A. Keith Bryan, Mr W. E. Hall, Mr W. Heap, Mrs Katharine Hooper, the late Mr C. B. Jewson, Miss R. H. Kamen of the library of the R.I.B.A.; Mrs S. M. Mills; there is an obituary in *The Builder* 21 June 1935, p.1142.

81 N. Jewson, *By Chance I Did Rove*, 1973, pp.1, 15. There is some interest in tracing pupils of Shaw, George, and Sedding. Arthur Keen, architect of Baptist Church House, Kingsgate Chapel and Anson Road Cricklewood, was a pupil of Norman Shaw; Ernest George's pupils included the Baptist R. H. Weymouth (d.1917), son of Dr Weymouth, Headmaster of Mill Hill School, 1869-85, and the Congregational Edward T. Boardman of Norwich (1861-1950, and himself an architect's son) whose sister was a sister-in-law of Norman Jewson.

82 I am grateful to Mr G. C. Greatham and Mr W. E. Hall for details of the work at Bishop's Stortford. N. Pevsner, *The Buildings of England: Cambridgeshire*, 1954, p.185.

83 R. G. Martin, *These Hundred Years: A Picture of Union Church, Hunstanton, 1870-1970* n.d. Hunstanton, *passim* esp.p.9.

84 I am grateful to the Revd A. K. Bryan for this information.

85 This section draws heavily upon W. Heap, *The Free Church (Baptist) Hillside Road Chorleywood and a History of its Architecture*. Open University B.A. Dissertation, 1976; and I am indebted to the minister of the church, the Revd Geoffrey Collins for guiding me around it.

86 Heap, op.cit. p.7.

87 Ibid. p.13.

88 Ibid.

89 There is another insensitivity: the carefully balanced impact of the
    pulpit end has been destroyed by the intrusion to one side of the organ.

90 *The Builder's Journal* 3 May 1905, p.238.

91 I am grateful to Miss Dorothy Gardner for information about Elmers End
    United Reformed Church.

92 *Appeal Brochure* for the proposed Elmers End Congregational Church.

93 Op.cit. See also C. Binfield, "Bridled Emotion", art.cit. pp.204-6;
    CYB 1931, p.211.

94 J.C.H., "A Master Builder"; cutting 29 June 1935, in possession of
    Revd A. K. Bryan.

95 Ibid.

96 Ibid.

97 H. G. Ibberson to Revd. Frank Bryan, 13 August 1917, in possession of
    Revd A. K. Bryan.

98 W. E. Orchard (1877-1955), then minister of King's Weigh House Congre-
    gational Church, London, previously a minister in the Presbyterian
    Church of England, and subsequently a Roman Catholic priest. Malcolm
    Spencer (1877-1950) then engaged in secretarial and literary work,
    previously with the Student Christian Movement, and subsequently (1925-
    48), Secretary of the Congregational Union's Social Service Committee.
    Like Spencer, Alan Knott (1889-1976), Elmers End's minister 1923-32,
    was an ecumenist with a social concern and their friendship may explain
    the choice of Ibberson as Elmers End's architect. Knott was reared a
    Baptist and had intended to train for the Baptist ministry, but he
    turned to Congregationalism and Mansfield College instead: *United
    Reformed Church Year Book*, 1977, p.268.

99 i.e. Bishop's Stortford College.

100 i.e. Lyndhurst Road Congregational Church, Hampstead, designed by Alfred
    Waterhouse and opened in 1884, where R. F. Horton (1855-1934) ministered
    until 1930.

101 The Quaker meeting house (and shrine) in Buckinghamshire.

102 On 11 August 1917, following the so-called "Doormat Incident", Arthur
    Henderson, the Labour politician, and minister without portfolio, had
    resigned from Lloyd George's War Cabinet.

103 *BHB* 1938, p.361.

104 G. W. Rusling, *Baptist Places of Worship*, 1965, p.5.

105 Ibid. p.6.

106 Ibid. p.18.

107 *Westgate Road Baptist Church: Jubilee Handbook*, op.cit. p.24.

108 Rusling, op.cit., p.6.

CLYDE   BINFIELD

St Andrew's Street Baptist Church, Cambridge (1903): "the assured, comfy, endearingly arty crafty Free Gothic of George Baines".

An artist's impression of Union Chapel, Islington:
breadth, space and largeness of parts.

The Church of the Redeemer, Hagley Road, Birmingham: James Cubitt's grandest Baptist church, opened in 1882.

The Church of the Redeemer - famous for its noble
size, its organ, and its draughts.

The preacher may be loud in addressing an audience;
he who prays cannot shout in addressing the Almighty.
The pulpit in James Cubitt's Church of the Redeemer.

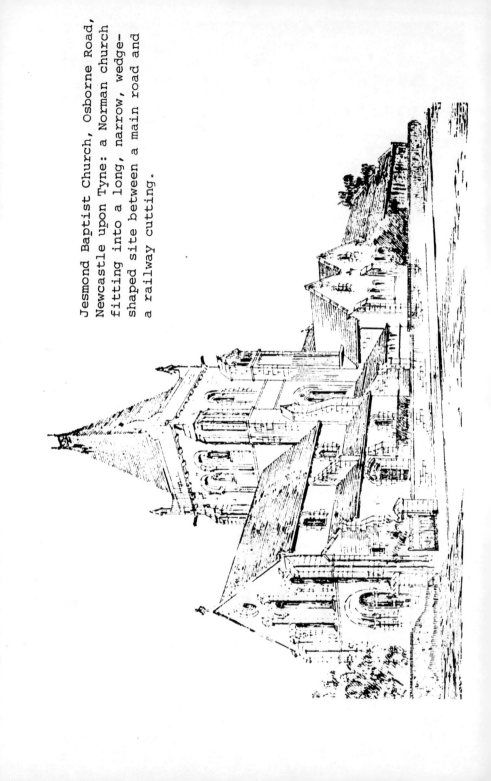

Jesmond Baptist Church, Osborne Road, Newcastle upon Tyne: a Norman church fitting into a long, narrow, wedge-shaped site between a main road and a railway cutting.

Jesmond Baptist Church, interior: the Chancel, a careful setting for the Puritan drama of Word and Sacrament.

H. J. Blanc's Thomas Coats Memorial Baptist Church, Paisley: the most ostentatious of all the rich men's Dissenting cathedrals.

The Meeting House of the Baptist Church at Chorley
Wood: H. G. Ibberson's unfulfilled intention,
grandly Free Gothic, and picturesquely roofed in
the everyday of Scotland, or England, or parts of
Germany, it is not clear which.

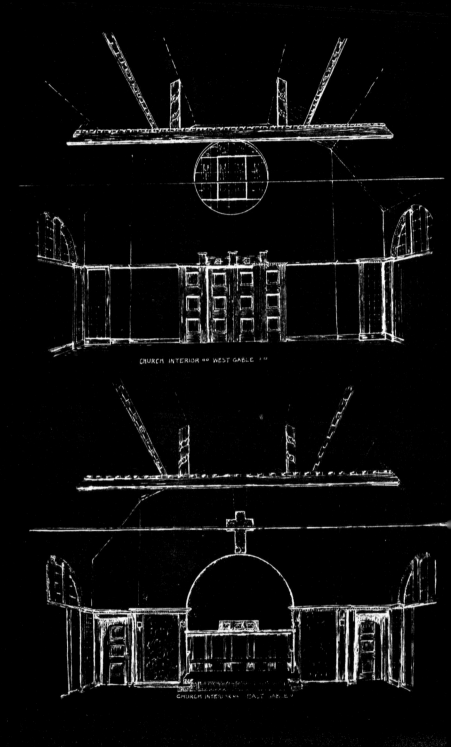

CHURCH INTERIOR -- WEST GABLE

CHURCH INTERIOR -- EAST GABLE

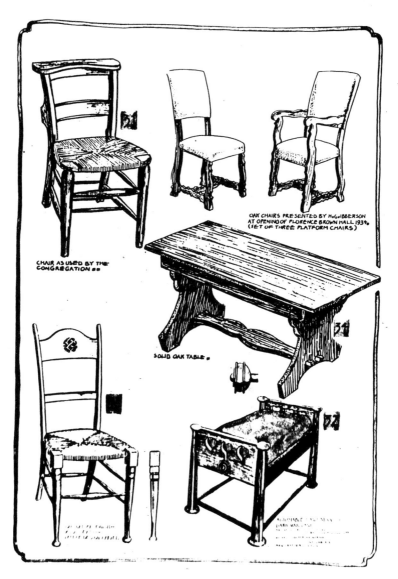

Within the illustration:

CHAIR AS USED BY THE CONGREGATION

OAK CHAIRS PRESENTED BY McGIBBERSON AT OPENING OF FLORENCE BROWN HALL 1939 (SET OF THREE PLATFORM CHAIRS)

SOLID OAK TABLE

Left. Drawings of the Chorley Wood Free Church's interior as built: an architectural use of colour and fabric dashingly rare in Free Churches.

Above. Free Church furniture, 'part country, part Voysey'.

Drawn by Mr W. Heap of Chorley Wood, and reproduced with his permission.

H. G. Ibberson's design for Elmers' End
Congregational Church: an unfinished essay
in texture and colour.

INDEX

Addicott, L., 85
Ainslie, Peter, 55
*Album of Northamptonshire Con-
gregational Churches*, 127
Aldwinkle, R., 68
Alexander, Viscount, 85
Allen, H., 22
Allon, Henry, 125
Amnesty International, 84
Amos, E., 110
Amsterdam Assembly, 59
Anabaptists, 31, 43
Angola, 84-5
Angus family (Newcastle), 126
Angus, Joseph, 21
Ashworth, Dr., 57-8
Aubrey, M.E., 58,60,83,86,88,
90,96,103,105-7,109-11
Minister's Manual, 6,23
Azariah, V.S., 58

Bailey, Gordon, 26
Bailey, Walter, 85
Baines, G. Palmer, 115,117,139n.
Baines, R. Palmer, 115
Baldwin, Stanley, 76
Baptism, 24-5,57-8,60-74,114
*Baptism, Confirmation and
Eucharist*, 70
Baptism, Eucharist and Ministry,
55,57,73
Baptists *passim.*
Baptist Associations
Bristol, 4
Glasgow, 17
Yorkshire, 42,80
Baptist Church Buildings
Ampthill, 131
Bath, Twerton, 116
Birmingham
Church of the Redeemer, 125,
128
Hamstead Road, 128
Moseley, 116
Oxford Road, 128
People's Chapel, 129
Wycliffe, 128
Cardiff, Hope, 134,137
Chorleywood, 131-2,137
Clacton, 115
Cricklewood, 116,140
Farnworth, 116
Frinton, 115
Hunstanton, 130,132
Hutton and Shenfield, 116

Baptist Church Buildings, cont.
Kingsgate, 115,128,140n.
Kirby Muxloe, 116
Ladbroke Grove, 120
Leavesden, 115
Leicester, Clarendon Hall, 115-6
Loughton, 140
Newcastle upon Tyne
Jesmond, 126
Rye Hill, 121,126
Westgate Road, 126,137
Wyclif, 139
Newhaven, 117
Nottingham, Woodborough Road, 115
Nuneaton, 117
Paisley, Coats Memorial, 126-8
Pembury, 115,122
Rawden, 115
Southport, 115
Spurgeon's, 122
West Ham, 115
Woking, 116
Baptist Church House, 115
Baptist Funds, 8
Baptist Handbook, 114-5
Baptist Historical Society, 1,43
Baptist Hymn Book, 26
Baptist Magazine, 21-2
Baptist Missionary Society, 12,84-5
Baptist Pacifist Fellowship, 84
Baptist Quarterly, 73
Baptist Times, 42,48,77-82,86-7,97-102,
105-7,109
Baptist Union, 4,12,21,31,36,39,43-4,
46-9,52,55-6,58,72,76-8,83-6,109-10
Baptist World Alliance, 50,57,84-5,
90,102-7,110-1
Barmen Confession, 98,105,107-9
Barnes, W.W., 56
Barnsley, Ernest, 118
Barnsley, Sidney, 118
Barth, Karl, 12,59-60,100,107-9
Beasley-Murray, G.R., 66,68
Baptism in the New Testament, 24-5
Bebbington, D.W.,
The Nonconformist Conscience, 11
Belcher, J., 129
Bell, G.K.A., 98
Bentley, J.F., 139n.
Berry, Sidney, 83
Bethge, E., 101
Bichkov, A.M., 90
Bidlake, George, 129
Bidlake, W.H., 129
Black, Cyril, 76,86